The Profound and the Profane

$\overline{X} \ \overline{IX} \ 96.$

Dear Steve

Happy Birthday.
I rather like this
guys angle on things.

All my LOVE
Chris

ALSO BY CHRISTOPHER TITMUSS

Spirit for Change (14 interviews on engaged spirituality),
Green Print, London, 1990.

Freedom of the Spirit (15 more interviews)
Green Print, London, 1991.

Spirit of Change (U.S. edition)
Hunter House Publishers, Alameda, Calif., 1992.

Fire Dance and other Poems
Insight Books, 1992.

Christopher Titmuss was ordained a Buddhist monk for six years
in Thailand and India from 1970-1976. He teaches spiritual awakening, engaged spirituality and insight meditation retreats
around the world.

He is the co-founder of Gaia House Trust, an insight meditation centre in Denbury, South Devon, England and the Sharpham
North Community, Ashprington, Totnes, Devon. Christopher is a
member of the international board of the Buddhist Peace Fellowship and is an active supporter of organizations working on global issues. He lives in Totnes. His daughter, Nshorna, attends the
local comprehensive school.

For information on retreats, teachings, contact
Gaia House Trust,
Denbury,
Newton Abbot,
Devon,
TQ12 6DY,
England.
Tel: +44-(0)803-813188.

The Profound and the Profane

AN INQUIRY INTO SPIRITUAL AWAKENING

Christopher Titmuss

edited by Gill Farrer-Halls

Insight Books (Totnes)

Insight Books (Totnes),
Sharpham Courtyard,
Ashprington,
Totnes,
Devon
TQ9 7UT
England.

Layout and design by Lewis Taylor
Cover design by Rick Lawrence

Insight Books is grateful to Micky Karlholm for
his support in financing the printing of this book.

ISBN 0 946672 27 X

A catalogue record for this book is available from the British
Library.

Printed and Bound in Great Britain
by Cromwell Press, Melksham, Wilts.

CONTENTS

ACKNOWLEDGMENTS

I can only name very few of many who have contributed to this book's publication. This expresses one of the main themes, that all people and situations arise dependent upon multiple conditions. Without the support of countless people neither book nor author would exist.

I regard the Dharma, the teachings of the Buddha, as making a significant contribution to understanding our life on Earth. I experience immense gratitude to the Buddha. In the West we like to compartmentalize teachings into such categories as religion, philosophy, psychology, sociology or politics. Yet the Dharma embraces all these and many more. I have endeavoured to state the significance of profound spiritual awakening and the issues and factors that inhibit realization. The presence of the Dharma shows in the teachings found in this book.

I wish to express my deep appreciation to Venerable Ajahn Dhammadharo, Abbot of Wat Sai Ngam (Monastery of Beautiful Banyan Trees), Supanburi, Thailand. I spent half of my six years as a Buddhist monk during 1970-73 in Wat Chai Na (Monastery at the End of the Rice Paddy) where Ajahn Dhammadharo was abbot at the time. He is a warrior for insight meditation, known as vipassana in the Buddhist tradition. He provided teachings and the environment there for me and other monks, nuns and lay people to face the bare actuality of our lives.

I also wish to express deep appreciation to Venerable Ajahn Buddhadassa of Wat Suanmoke (Monastery of the Garden of Liberation), Chai Ya, Thailand. Ajahn Buddhadassa has given teachings unceasingly for more than 60 years without fear or favour. I spent a year in the forest with him and learnt much from him about the Dharma of life.

I also wish to thank Gwanwyn Williams, our daughter Nshorna, also my mother and late father for their support.

. Gill Farrer-Halls, a former member of Sharpham Community, Totnes, has read each draft. I appreciate her editing skills and firm comments. I also wish to thank Sharda (Henrietta Rogell) who read through the first draft of the typescript. Lewis Taylor kindly prepared the layout and text for publication and Rick Lawrence designed the jacket. Thanks also to the Buddhist Publishing

Group for practical assistance.

Many thanks and gratitude to the Theravada and Mahayana Buddhist traditions, Ajahn Po, AMECO, Maurice Ash, The Barn, Beethoven, Steve Biko, William Blake, Bodh Gaya, Bodhi Farm, Buddhist Peace Fellowship, Sally Clough, Daisy Bate, David Arnott, Dan Clurman, Rose Deiss, Dalai Lama, Dharma Seed Tape Library, Bob Dylan, T.S.Eliot, Christina Feldman, CIMC, Meister Eckhart, Erich Fromm, Mahatma Gandhi, Martine Batchelor, Judy Fox, Gaia House, the Green Party, Guy Armstrong, Hunter House, INEB, Inquiring Mind, Insight Meditation Society, Insight Tapes, Isabel Marto, Jesus, Jon Carpenter, John Keats, the Guylers, Anne Kelly, Katie Mitchell, Kho Pha-Ngan, Krishnamurti, D.H. Lawrence, Karl Marx, Meichee Patomwon, Murray Feldman, Nagarjuna, the Nature, New Addington, Norman Feldman, Pali Suttas, Judy Phillips, Ramana Maharshi, Relative Truth, Rilke, Roman Catholic Church, San Francisco-Bay area sangha, Schumacher College, Shanti, Sharpham Trust, Sharpham Community, Strunk and White, Sgt. Pepper, Socrates, St. John of the Cross, State of the World, Stephen Batchelor, Sutta Nipata, Swami Dayananda, Peggy Swan, Thai Monastery, Thich Nhat Hahn, Thomas Jost, Trees, Ultimate Truth, Fred Von Allmen, Wildlife, Waldhaus, Yvonne Weier, Ludwig Wittgenstein, Vimalo, Don Whitbread, people of Totnes, lovers of Dharma in Thailand and India—and the melting snowflakes.

May all people, animals and environment live in peace and harmony.

INTRODUCTION

Our society glosses over deeply rooted problems including self-ishness, fear and aggression. These problems are regarded as normal forms of human behaviour. We are blind to our intransigent attitudes, cynicism and degradation of spiritual values. We have become obsessed with consumer goods and status and put a price on everything. We may feel helpless in the face of our own problems let alone global issues.

The purpose of this book is to inquire into ourselves and our values for the genuine welfare and awakening of ourselves and society. Authentic spiritual experience reveals a profoundly liberating sense of wisdom with a deep and active reverence for all life. In this book I have explored facets of the spiritual life, and have presented an overview of daily life from a liberated viewpoint. Each section and chapter is a statement of my understanding of issues in the light of insights I have had over the years. I have not hesitated to question and challenge sacred cows of both religious and secular life.

I have examined issues affecting our lives such as desire, death, belief, the notion of self, concepts of God, meditation and liberation. I have questioned authority again and again. The majority of our religious and political leaders show little genuine reverence for life and prefer to cling instead to their respective ideologies. I have inquired into our inter-dependence with each other and the natural world. I have written of the necessity for an expansive and active awareness.

This book is a contribution to spiritual awakening. It explores the forces that corrupt the luminosity of the mind and the world. Concern with agreement or disagreement is missing the raison d'être of the book. Our existence is an opportunity to abide with wisdom and compassion, joy and celebration. Rather than remaining trapped in dogmatic views and fixed habits, we must learn to take risks to discover something "other" that is all too often missing from our lives.

I am not interested in converting you to my set of views nor in reinforcing your own. At times you may well come across passages that you cannot agree with. That, of course, is your right and privilege. When that happens I would suggest you close the book and reflect on your response so that differences of perception and understanding are not a cause for hurried rejection or conflict.

Throughout the text I have examined the influence of thought, which we have come to believe functions objectively outside of the nature of things. As prisoners of thought, we treat life as a means to sustain our rigid views, and pursue our daydreams and ambitions. Thought has no inherent or objective existence but frequently emerges out of the force of circumstances and the pattern of past conditioning. Awakening transforms our way of thinking about our presence in the Here and Now.

This book provides a resource for inquiry, spiritual exploration and liberating insights, but if this book is to be a vehicle for transformation, it is vital that the reader keep faith with some fundamental questions about himself or herself. "How does this relate to my life?" "What views do I cherish?" "Am I willing to be aware and respond to what is unsatisfactory within me and around me?" "What risks am I prepared to take to be a free human being?" "What am I willing to give up to serve others?" Sustaining such questions will safeguard the reader from reading with only intellectual interest. In this way the book can bring immediate insight and awakening.

Awakening transforms our heart, our thought realms and even our cells so that we express awareness and wisdom in the world. The touch of the ineffable, the grace of infinite discovery is often assumed to be a rare privilege. I believe all human beings have the potential to experience realization of the Vast and Inexpressible. Such sublime experiences reveal an eternal freshness that breaks the spell of mechanical existence; this awakening to Ultimate Truth lies at the heart of an enlightened way of being in the world. There is a revelation of the immeasurable capacity of human beings to transcend narrow self interest. Such realizations affect us in the very depths of our being. Enlightenment reveals a range of liberating insights, not only into the Ultimate Truth of things, but also into the conventions of everyday life.

There appears to be no precondition for transcendent realizations—in moments of joy or fear, meditative calmness or turbulence, action or stillness, alone or with others. Transcendence sweeps aside notions of an isolated self existence. Such impeccable sweetness uplifts our whole sense of being beyond the trivial and the familiar, thus effortlessly accommodating Heaven and Earth.

Perhaps the most well known recorded case of awakening is the experience that happened to Gautama Siddhartha, more than 2500 years ago. Gautama the Buddha claimed enlightenment to the Ultimate Truth in Bodh Gaya, Bihar, India. He underwent a series of realizations about the nature of life, culminating in understanding ultimate wisdom, liberation and the place of conventional experience. It is necessary to understand that enlightenment is neither the intensity nor immediacy of the impact of an experience but what manifests in the world. It is the actions of an enlightened person that are significant not their personal claims nor their admirers.

The "language" of enlightenment or awakening reveals itself through the hearts of those who have "eyes" to see. No particular language can ever communicate the state of enlightenment. Some people are perceptive and can articulate their realizations; others remain silent or, in a rather clumsy manner, perhaps understandable to them alone, speak of the eternal mystery of things that defies intellectual comprehension. They spend their lives in an active appreciation of that transcendence untainted by events. Enlightened people, including Buddhas, are not perfect. They are not always clear in every moment, or in every expression of body, speech and mind. But their unsatisfactory thoughts and states of mind are rare.

The language employed by the vast reservoir of teachers, traditions and books varies considerably. Some express their experiences in the language of their religion while others use a personal form of language. Both need to be acknowledged and respected. Yet a particular experience, event or language does not define awakening. There is no necessity for a special moment—the realization of Ultimate Truth may not be dramatic. There are those who cannot recall such a major event yet they manifest ultimate realizations, not through claims to a particular form of spiritual experience but through their liberated way of being in the world.

Untainted by narrow self interest and actively expressing freedom, such people may disregard such words as awakening or enlightenment, and never conceive of themselves in that privileged category. They may have never entertained the thought of being enlightened. It is not even necessary to *think* in such categories. Sometimes those who claim to be enlightened have displayed extreme forms of the narrow mind, conceit or arrogance that would not be tolerated outside of a religion.

Those who think they are enlightened may ask themselves: "Can I be enlightened if I do not conceive of myself in that way?" The answer might be found in engaging in several honest meditative reflections. By exploring different areas of our relationship to existence, we can find our meaning of awakening rather than it being a nebulous concept belonging exclusively to the province of great spiritual masters.

There is a range of spiritual experiences: there are the insights that emerge from them and there is their application in our daily life. I regard awakening as embracing all three facets of realization not just the first or second. Each section and each chapter in "The Profound and the Profane" points to a Freedom in life that cannot be measured. No tradition binds the teachings in this book, but the book is not written at the expense of those who experience reverence for their spiritual tradition.

The following areas need to be understood or explored when considering the nature of enlightenment.

An enlightened human being has realized the Ultimate Truth. There are no doubts, no ambivalence and no forgetfulness of its liberating significance.

What are the liberating insights that have emerged out of the realization?

Is there recognition and appreciation in the Here and Now of the Ultimate Truth where suffering has no hold?

An enlightened human being is devoted to ending suffering in this world, to serving others and has renounced self-centred existence. An enlightened human is wise, happy and fearless.

What is the relationship to the five ethical foundations, briefly explored in the opening chapter? Each one of these areas—not killing, not stealing, not sexually violating others, not lying, nor engaging in alcohol and drug abuse—embraces a respectful and non-dual relationship to others as well as oneself.

This ethical basis is integral to all circumstances of living with wisdom. To disregard deliberately any of the five ethics leads to suffering. Such patterns of destructive behaviour obscure awakening—although ignoring these principles for living wisely does not deny a wide range of secondary spiritual experiences.

Do I ever fall into the hell realms? The hell realms are states of mind such as depression, obsessive addictions, megalomania and self hate? Can I become so angry that I am capable of inflicting physical violence on others? An awakened person is free from falling into such states of mind, but those who suffer from them can also have a wide range of spiritual experiences.

What is my relationship to all that I call the personality? Am I so wrapped up in selfishness and identification with what I want for myself that I can rarely, if at all, see beyond it?

What is my relationship to authority, religious services, rites, spiritual practices and techniques? Is there dependency? Do I believe that such practices, with the accompanying forms and language, have some inherent significance? How can dependency on such involvement lead to liberation that frees me from dependency upon such activities?

Enlightenment reveals a contented and compassionate heart free from pain and the suffering of greed, violence, fear and anxiety.

Spiritual experiences of joy and ecstasy, though invaluable may not necessarily have any lasting impact on consciousness and our way of perceiving and acting. The true nature of enlightenment is when the insights into Ultimate Truth are actualized in our daily lives. This enlightenment includes a wondrous sense of Emptiness of separate or self-existence and a non-dual participation in circumstances.

Some readers will recognize the influence of the Buddhist tradition throughout these pages. For example, the opening chapter concerns the five ethical guidelines—familiar to everyone connected with Buddhism. The second chapter explores mindfulness of breathing, a spiritual practice common to all Buddhist traditions. The insights of the Buddha, his foremost commentator, Nagarjuna, and the insight meditation (vipassana) tradition, have contributed significantly to my understanding. But I have never forgotten that teachers, traditions and practices belong to a time-bound world. I have no wish to promote any particular religious tradition since all require the same penetrative eye of caring and critical exploration as any other body of teachings. Ultimate Truth dissolves the confines of views that inhibit our liberation.

Realising the Emptiness of clinging onto people, beliefs and things, you will feel concern for those who suffer through such forms of dependency and attachments. You will find a way to express your compassion for others, for animals and the environment because you have awakened to the factors that contribute to suffering. From the Ultimate Truth of things, you will effortlessly commit yourself to an active reverence for life. Once you have realized spiritual enlightenment, a heartfelt liberation, and active concern for others, there is no possibility of turning back to self-centred existence.

May all beings live in peace
May all beings live in harmony
May all beings be awakened.

Part One
Relationship to the World

CHAPTER ONE

THE "GOOD" AND THE "NOT GOOD"

The damaged Earth and most of its inhabitants are sliding towards Hell. Human behaviour contributes to this nightmare of hardship and terror let loose upon the world. We pay little respect to ethics and the quality of our inner life and how we manifest in the world. Unacknowledged and unresolved problems of the human psyche tear into the fabric of existence. Many people live in a spiritual vacuum and express indifference if not contempt for religion. Few people have access to spiritual experiences, and even when spiritual experiences occur, they make little impact on day-to-day life. Friends, family and society often dismiss or ridicule those who experience genuine spiritual insights.

Yet centuries ago different religious people who were also socially aware shared insights that could enable human beings to live peacefully together. These insights formed the foundations for harmony in social life and for liberating inquiry into the nature of things. The wise said repeatedly that a sane and just society is based upon respect for these guidelines. Thoughtful people still agree that it is "good" to observe these guidelines and "not good" to ignore them owing to the suffering that ensues. To get the point over to the people, spiritual teachers would speak of these insights as basic codes for right action or as commandments of God. Though they vary from culture to culture, these insights are often expressed as:

I undertake not to engage in killing.
I undertake not to engage in stealing.
I undertake not to engage in sexual abuse.
I undertake not to engage in lying.
I undertake not to engage in abuse of alcohol and drugs.

These guidelines were often designated moral laws to protect human beings from inflicting pain upon each other and themselves. Religious people upheld them despite conflicting social and national values since they held nonviolence and nonexploitation above other considerations. Today, as in times past, many claim to uphold these insights but neglect them when personal, social or national aims become more important. We switch our viewpoint when we agree to:

wage war,
go for what we want,
enjoy sex regardless of another's feelings,
speak without regard for facts, and
pursue abuse of alcohol and drugs.

What is good and what is not good does not remain fixed and these ethics need to be interpreted and used skilfully in the ever changing circumstances of daily life. If we are feeling comfortable with our ethical behaviour it may show our ineptitude at examining the various ways we reject or modify these five guidelines with an alarming degree of frequency. Yet we are prone to judging other people for neglecting these social values. It is easy to condemn the murderer, thief, rapist, liar and addict when we do not understand the circumstances and history of the individual and their environment.

The first guideline: Not engaging in killing.
Violating the first guideline is having the intention to kill and killing the person(s).

There are five ways to kill:
killing through physical contact,
killing with a weapon or instrument,
killing through mental domination (e.g. causing somebody to commit suicide),
killing through the law,
killing through giving orders.

Both wisdom and fear may inhibit us from killing or inflicting pain on another or others. We may not even find ourselves involved in situations where the intention would arise, so this guideline is often upheld without the test of circumstances.

The greatest test of our commitment to the first guideline is in times of war or when under personal attack. We are vulnerable to leaders who manipulate our emotions through jingoism and regional chauvinism. Leaders justify the killing of others for the nation by disregarding the morality of the first guideline. Many religious leaders remain passive while politicians declare war; others justify bombing, bless the military, invoke capital punishment and make a mockery of nonviolent principles. Passages in religious books support national aims and exhort violence. Circumstances of danger and violation then condone killing others; thus national interests support destruction of life, terrorism and violence. The inability to resolve issues through communication and insight contributes to the various scenes of aggression, fear, and greed acted out on the world stage.

Respect for the first guideline has a more significant role to play in world affairs than religion. If the first guideline was observed, there would be no need for the military and no expenditure on arms. Poverty would not exist and people would not live in terror of each other.

When we or our loved ones are threatened we cannot say how we will act. Speculating about hypothetical situations is unsatisfactory; the champions of nonviolence for all their talk may react violently when threatened, while the champions of the "eye for an eye" belief also may respond differently from how they imagine.

Not killing can include our relationship to animals, birds and fish. Countless millions are consumed at meals, experimented upon in laboratories, killed for sport and pleasure, and stripped of their skins and fur for clothing and ornaments. What are our views in these areas? Religious authorities rarely concern themselves with animal welfare. They claim that animals do not have souls and exist for our use. Such religious views become a rationalization for uncaring and insensitive treatment of other species, who can communicate but not articulate their pain.

The charge of romantic idealism is often aimed at those who uphold nonkilling above personal and national considerations and these critics probably speak with at least a grain of truth. But those who uphold killing as a means to stop killing, even when sanctioned by the state, abide equally in the realms of idealism. To imagine that the answer to the end of killing is taking more life is equally bizarre.

The second guideline: Not engaging in forms of theft.
There are two distinct ways in which stealing occurs. The first is
the deliberate intention to remove something that belongs to
another person, people or organization without consulting the
owner and to keep it without their agreement. The second is
using means such as fraud, embezzlement, blackmail, swindling,
or deception to cheat others. These are various forms of tampering with other people's assets to get or retain what does not
belong to the taker.

Forgery, tampering with accounts, false use of weights and
measures, unreasonably hiking up the cost and dishonesty are
strategies of the greedy, where the desire for money, goods or
land overshadows ethical considerations. Severe poverty may
force individuals to steal for themselves and their families, thus
stealing must be understood in its relationship to circumstances.
The action of stealing includes:

the deliberate intention to steal,

knowledge that the property or money belongs to others,

*the act of removing the items concerned, whether by ourselves or
through giving directions to another.*

Undertaking to be free from any form of stealing also challenges our whole notion of honesty and integrity. We cleverly
maximize investments through ignoring a corporation's activities. A business may cheat others out of their payments, goods,
lands or rights. Hypnotized by figures businesses and individuals juggle money to make a fast buck. Investors will support
major corporations who exploit people and land in the Third
World. Profits accrue on the backs of cheated workers and those
made redundant. Investors engage in stock market gambling to
add a few more figures to their bank account. Personal profit
becomes a form of theft when we deprive others of what right-
fully belongs to them.

The difference between those in desperate need of money and
those who are not must be examined. We all share responsibility
for the division between rich and poor. Water, food, clothing, a
home and medicine are basic human rights for all. Respect for the
second guideline gives support for the cheated and dispossessed.

Feelings of insecurity, often from lack of spiritual values, force
us to pursue prosperity at the expense of others. The acquisition
of wealth while bending the law hits the under privileged, but in

modern Western society cleverness and greed have become inter-
changeable values. We are destroying the world not through lack
of knowledge but through greed and insecurity. We have become
too clever for everybody's good.

The first two prescriptions for social harmony, not killing and
not stealing, often share a close relationship. The dismissal of the
second guideline can lend itself, directly or indirectly, to disregard of the first.

The third guideline: Not engaging in sexual abuse.
Sexual abuse, whether heterosexual or homosexual, occurs
through rape, incest and abusive manipulation of another
engaged in a committed monogamous relationship.

A person may become sexually involved with another owing
to the forces of attraction but this does not necessarily violate the
third precept. There are differences for consenting adults between
sexual communion and sexual abuse. Sexual abuse is the physical
violation of another to gain personal satisfaction. Violation of
another occurs through acting against their wishes, taking advantage of that person when he or she is unable to respond. This
would apply to adults who are emotionally insecure, children,
mentally handicapped or intoxicated people as well as those who
resist sexual activity.

Sexual abuse also occurs through exploitation of privilege by
those in charismatic roles or the helping professions which result
in direct harm to another. Sexual abuse also can take place against
a person, who is experiencing a time of emotional vulnerability.

The religious idea that sex is sinful before marriage is the view
of those attached to models of behaviour. They claim the
sequence of engagement, marriage and sex is necessary to keep
family life sacred. Others, deeply committed to spiritual life,
regard engagement and marriage as a social contract, bearing no
spiritual significance. Some religious and political authorities
condemn sexual intimacy outside marriage and the right of the
gay and lesbian community to live with the same gender. These
also are expressions of attachments to models of behaviour, but
homosexual or heterosexual activity has no inherent relationship
to unsatisfactory sexual behaviour. The circumstances of the sexual act has to be considered not gender.

A sexual relationship can have a long term impact on our emotional life and requires much sensitivity. Consideration before intimacy is vital. If sexual contact makes another suffer, either at the time or later, then the issue of behaviour may arise. Sexual intimacy between a man and a woman can *very* easily lead to the conception of a child, which, if unwanted, leads to suffering.

Sexuality is potent and needs our understanding, care and insight.

Casual sex can involve taking advantage of another's emotional or economic realities.

Secret sex outside a committed relationship may contribute to fear, paranoia or heartbreak.

Unresolved sexual needs contribute to abuse of personal power.

The advertising industry exploits sexual needs to sell its products.

With the widespread number of sexually transmitted diseases, sex as a health factor deserves widespread public attention.

Rough behaviour makes a mockery of sensitive sexual passion. Repressed sexual desire is dangerous and when it surfaces can cause pain for self and others. Self knowledge, communication with both genders, comfort with sexual feelings and meditation guard against sexual mistreatment of others. When we are at ease with sexuality we are less likely to be caught up in the celibacy-marriage conflict common to religious beliefs.

The fourth guideline: Not speaking lies.

This guideline is undertaking to speak the truth, to stop the lies that give misleading impressions. Factors to be considered in lying to another or others are:

intention to deceive,

the consequences of the lie,

the rationalization given to support the lie,

the profit in the lie.

Social, economic and emotional factors all affect the quality of speech. We easily enter into false speech through misrepresentation, slander, backbiting, gossip and half-truths. Exaggerations and distortions undermine the truth. We create fictional accounts of events to serve our personal ends which we repeat until we ourselves believe them. We then no longer know the difference between what is fact and what is fiction.

Sometimes we speak like journalists who admit to "never letting the truth stand in the way of a good story." Or politicians who imply: "We've made up our minds so don't confuse us with the facts." Both want to make an impression and generate an image so the meaning of words becomes a tool for propaganda. Fear of punishment or retribution often forces adults and children to tell lies. Anxiety and pressure affect the ability to think clearly, to be honest and state the facts. Such people may not wilfully play around with the truth; they are afraid to speak out owing to the consequences for themselves or others. Circumstances often dictate what is said or written. The words we choose and the meanings we give them are born from immediate considerations. Experience, perception, behaviour and vested interests influence what we say and write.

A common form of false speech is backbiting. We seem to derive some weird pleasure from slagging others off or praising them heavens high behind their backs. From generating negative or positive images about the person or group, we can succeed in convincing another our view is genuine. We need to convince others, reinforce our position and convert another person to our projections.

In all situations the lie depends upon others for its acceptance. It is co-dependent on the believer for the lie to be established, so when we blame only the liar we fail to look at the Totality of the situation. Lying violates other ethics when the consequences of the lie are harmful to ourselves or others. Right speech, like the other four guidelines, asks us to engage in mindful consideration of our impulses and distorted perceptions. Mindfulness protects us from creating unhealthy reactions to circumstances and invites us to look into our patterns of behaviour, to understand ourselves and treat others as we wish to be treated. We then discover the opportunity to affirm the well-being and self-respect of ourselves and others.

The fifth guideline: Not abusing drugs or alcohol.
Alcohol is socially acceptable in western society. Some forms of mind altering drugs are acceptable in other societies and in the western counter cultures. Whether socially acceptable or unacceptable, excessive use of alcohol and drugs is a major social issue. Alcohol and drugs distort everyday mental perceptions and contribute to careless acts of body, speech and mind. Abstinence is often the only alternative to alcohol and drug abuse.

Personal, social, economic and political considerations can all influence our behaviour so that we start to engage in substance abuse leading to the misery of addiction. Conditions for addiction include boredom, insecurity, pressure from peers, desire to impress, habit, poverty, loneliness, suffering and hereditary factors.

People of all ages and backgrounds are vulnerable to alcohol and drugs. The capacity of the drug (legal and illegal) and alcohol industries to play on the vulnerability of people has established a widespread global problem. For example, when an advertising agency wanted to market a whisky, the agency called in several alcoholics asking them to choose the advertising photograph that made them feel most thirsty. The alcoholics chose a photograph of an open bottle of whisky standing beside a glass with ice cubes. The agency launched a highly successful international campaign using that photograph.

The danger with abstinence is the tendency to moralize and repress desire. Manufacturers of alcohol try to convince us that drink is necessary to enjoy ourselves. The emotional, intellectual and biological consequences of alcohol addiction needs to be highlighted so that the true cost of alcohol is evident. Knowing the difference between use and abuse of alcohol is recognizing what part it plays in our life. In the abuse of alcohol, carelessness and violence are never far away. Alcohol can be a respite from isolation and despair, but like drugs, the bottle is a poor substitute for genuine hospitality and friendship.

Some illegal drugs alter consciousness. Soft and hard drugs may usher in some insight and religious experience, even a turning point in inner awareness but they do not liberate human beings from greed and fear. The hippie revolution spawned a field day for drug barons and dealers who continue to rake in huge profits at the expense of users and abusers. The tobacco industry promotes addiction to cigarettes and cigars making millions servants of the drug. This industry succeeds in destroying the health and lives of their victims who die agonizingly from various cancers and other smoking related diseases. Suffering is rarely personal; loved ones also suffer at a friend's or relative's addiction, sickness, or death. Legal, prescribed drugs, tea and coffee deserve attention, too. The human organism is a refined instrument, able to tolerate a moderate use of alcohol and drugs but abuse of any substance causes suffering.

Occasional indulgence in mind altering drugs may seem inconsequential so we absolve ourselves from any responsibility. We continue to smoke, inhale, sniff, swallow and inject substances. We take up religious rhetoric from ancient spiritual traditions to support playing with mind altering drugs. The capacity to say "no" to abuse, and even to use, is a human right. Through co-operation with others we can discover ways to stop harmful habits and experience the freedom of a wise and healthy way of living.

These foundations for living with wisdom benefit ourselves and others. When we apply these values we live with a degree of happiness and contentment not available to those who ignore them. Mindfulness and freedom from confusion protects our wellbeing and supports ethical values. Delighting in the challenge to lead as clear an ethical life as our understanding permits, we can reflect on our way of being in the world. We must recognize whether we grasp ethical concerns to judge others. Moralizing shows a prejudiced mind, a belief in self-righteousness and distorted values.

In a caring social philosophy these guidelines serve the genuine welfare of all. Thus ethical development is linked to spiritual awareness and wisdom. Contemplation of our actions for the welfare of all living beings reminds us that we participate in a global and nondual life. Then we do not react to circumstances from narrow self interest or national interests. The intention not to harm others is wisdom at work. We understand the nature of pain. We are arresting the slide towards hell.

CHAPTER TWO

REMEMBERING TO BREATHE

Perhaps drawing in the first inhalation of air at birth is the first significant experience of a human being. The release of the newborn into the environment ends nine months of physical restraint. The life force expands and contracts rhythmically. Chest, throat and nostrils inhale and exhale, gently or rapidly, but becoming stronger. The human process is under way.

The exhalation of air might be our last significant experience. At the point of death our body heat, faculties and consciousness enter the final cooling. The breath disappears into obscurity as the body loses its capacity to suck in any air. The human process is fading away. Between these two poles of arrival and departure of human life, the dance of circumstantial existence gives shape to life. Intentions, states of mind and environment become major influences.

The respiration hardly merits interest unless entering extremes—the fast pounding chest when running, or its slow heave in the time of immense happiness or sadness, or the sublime quietude of rest. An outstanding respiration, noticeable by a sudden change in sensations, grabs the attention only to settle back to its normal pattern. Usually it does not merit making a fuss over. What possible application could mindfulness of breathing have to our lives? Isn't the function of respiration simply to keep us alive? Yet could this facet of existence, as it changes through the stream of experiences, be a key to awakening? The word *spiritual* has its origins in the Latin *spiritualis*—of breathing. —to abide in an enlightened and enlivened way.

Could mindfulness of breathing be a resource for human welfare as valuable as the lush life of the tropical rain forest, as protective as the ozone layer, and as insightful as the scientist's penetrative gaze through the microscope? Direct application of mindfulness of breathing, gross or subtle, to a range of circumstances enables us to find out. When faced with challenging circumstances, we naturally take a deep inhalation—an instinctive reaction. Conscious breathing gives access to inner resources to deal with difficult situations. The air element sustains us as much as food and water. We can only survive three minutes without air before the living organism goes into a cataclysm of dysfunctioning and rapidly dies.

Mindfulness of breathing is a resource to work with the pleasures and pains of body and mind. It has a calming influence on consciousness. Directing attention to the breath brings calm and insight. Remembering to breathe mindfully expresses a simple act of discrimination. Exercised regularly through the day, conscious inhaling and exhaling focuses the mind steadfastly in the Here and Now. The Here and Now is a remarkable resource for clear attunement to life. Remembering to breathe becomes a meaningful exercise safeguarding the mind from wandering unnecessarily and excessively into the worlds of senses and events.

The common patterns of mental distraction, such as day dreaming and fantasizing, can cease when we are focusing on the air element. No matter how far the mind may wander, no matter how indulgent in superficial and cursory thought, air is never more than a thought away. The respiration serves as an anchor for the mind strung out on ideas alienated from the realities of the present.

The spiritual practice of mindfulness of breathing interrupts unsatisfactory patterns of behaviour and selfish interests including creative, social and economic considerations. The wisdom of choosing to breathe through a wave of desire acts to dispel the wave. Then desire does not so easily gain a foothold. In the dissolution of selfish desire we express awareness of its consequence to ourselves, our circumstances and others. Dissolution or moderation of the appetite for excess protects the Earth and its inhabitants. Mindfulness of breathing restrains the excesses of attraction and aversion. Interruption of the desire gives thought a second chance to pursue or harass the object of interest—or let it go.

In this respect, mindfulness of breathing is a useful contribution for a sustainable and harmonious society. Unsatisfactory mental patterns wither away when inhalations and exhalations act as a respite from the plague of the wanting mind. The force of desire knows no limit, cannot curb itself. No amount of thoughts seems to dissolve desire when it is under way. By switching attention to the respiration and away from personal pursuits, consciousness itself, so to speak, has a chance to breathe. Whether it requires a handful of conscious breaths, or a considerable number, it is not a waste of time to minimize the cravings and the obsessive infatuations in the overwhelming hunt for satisfaction.

The validity of mindfulness of breathing not only applies to the pursuit of the desirable but also when resisting the undesirable such as moments of fear, excitement, tiredness or stress. This spiritual practice needs to be applied when we are sitting, walking, standing, bending, stretching, lying down and getting up. All postures offer equal opportunity to remember to breathe. The air element becomes a friend, a point of access, immediate, reliable, an undemanding presence waiting to be converted into an agent for inner change. Mindfulness of breathing, when accompanied by realization, becomes Godlike in its power to transform events—to make the blind within ourselves see and the deaf within to listen. It enables us to find the faith to move mountains of fear and to walk on clear calm waters in a world drowning in negative emotions.

Allegiance to religious beliefs may not provide support for handling mood swings; mindfulness of breathing can become a cornerstone for coping with confusion. Spiritual practice is not supernatural, but we should heed its remarkable capacity to extricate consciousness from confusion, and respect its profound potential for liberating us from the tyranny of merciless thought. Mindfulness of breathing acts as a catalyst for understanding the potency of thought in the conventional world. A steady, relaxed focus on inhaling and exhaling reveals a state beyond thought. It's a dissolution of the trivial, the bothersome and the mundane—a boundless moment. Perhaps no meditation object is so effective in clearing away the muddied waters of desires and simultaneously offering a liberating vision. We realize the significance of the Here and Now.

Mindfulness of breathing can be used as a resource for calmness and clarity wherever our location. It also can be a meditation object while sitting in a formal posture in a quiet and still environment. This means the meditator engages in a sustained mode of formal spiritual practice. This approach, widely adopted for many centuries in the East, has guidelines that facilitate the presence of a meditative awareness. Guidance from a teacher is helpful for beginners, particularly for those interested in extended periods of this spiritual practice.

Here are some basic guidelines. Sit with a straight back. Keep the eyes closed with the eyelids just resting. If tired then keep the eyes open gently observing the ground one or two metres ahead. Initially breathe deeply to experience some sense of expansion in the chest, diaphragm and stomach area. This expands the lungs and takes pressure off some organs such as liver, kidney, and spleen. It allows blood and air to circulate more easily.

Allow the whole body to relax so that the tension required to maintain the posture is negligible. It makes no difference whether we sit in a chair, cross legged, or kneel using a small bench designed for meditation. The shape of our legs in the sitting posture has no relevance to meditation. Having made a clear intention to undertake this spiritual practice, direct the attention to the respiratory process. Experience the air as it passes into the nostrils, goes past the throat and down into the lungs. With inhalation the chest expands and with exhalation the chest contracts. Be with the experience without using force or will power.

If it is useful, make long breaths in a relaxed and comfortable manner. Once settled, allow the air to come and go in its natural rhythm. At times the respiration is likely to be quite short, hardly discernible, sometimes very distinct and almost tangible. Notice the different bodily sensations as the air flows into the organism; notice how far it goes down into the body.

At times, moments may go by before the next inhalation and after the last exhalation. Remain in that state of quiet repose, patiently, trusting in the body to inhale. Through familiarity with the process, attention naturally expands to include not only the specific areas between nose, chest and abdomen but the entire body. By inhaling and exhaling through the whole body we experience calmness. At this point a clear, relaxed intention to abide calmly contributes directly to its outcome.

Mindfulness of breathing may give access to sublime joy and happiness as the heart, mind, body and breath begin to harmonize together. There is no need to pursue a special experience for the priority is to keep in touch with the immediate experience. (Old Buddhist texts describe joy as the sight of fresh water to a thirsty person. Happiness is the tasting of such water).

While engaged in this spiritual practice there will be periods, (which often means much of the time) when the breath is not the object of attention. Everything else is more interesting. Like a chattering monkey jumping agitatedly in a cage, the mind will behave similarly with little ability to rest with the air element. Patterns of restlessness and habits of indulging in moods and streams of fantasy often sabotage sustainable contact with the practice.

Diversions away from the breath matter as much as being with it. They offer a chance to learn about the patterns and directions of an inattentive mind. We can develop the capacity to acknowledge and understand the range of our experiences. While connecting with the breath is the priority, streams of thoughts and fantasies provide the meditator with insights into the personality structure. At times contact with inhaling and exhaling triggers a range of strong emotions. It can be a struggle to try to force ourselves to return to mindfulness of breathing.

Acknowledgment of the emotions by remaining open to them is important. An appropriate attitude is allowing waves of strong feelings to arise and pass. When it feels appropriate we return to mindfulness of breathing. Commitment to observation of experiences instead of identification with them safeguards us from having to act them out. Consciousness suffusing the air element, through attention, in turn suffuses the mental state. The mind comes to quietude. Such attention strips away the layers of roles and identities that have accumulated and through which the ego gains substance. Mindfulness of breathing reveals what is present—thoughts, emotions, habits—but also what is not present. There is a liberating opportunity to appreciate the Emptiness of egotism and the notion that it possesses an unchanging and substantial existence.

Our various roles and identities do not have continual presence; events great and small constantly interrupt them. Mindfulness of breathing shows us that the roles and identities are empty of any self existence. They arise when the conditions are there for them to occur. One conscious breath dispenses with the most egotistical fantasy in that moment. Ego lacks continuity. Ongoing roles and identities do not have the relevance we imagine. Insight dispels myths around roles revealing roles as mental constructions, arising and passing in particular situations. Free from obsessing around our roles, we sense our full participation in the Here and Now.

The ego constructs itself around name, birth, age, roles, family, money, nationality, gender, beliefs and knowledge. These signposts of self are irrelevant to inner awakening. Who we are, what we are, what we have done and what we identify with are as irrelevant in awakening as they are in sleep. Sustained mindfulness of breathing exposes the Emptiness of endless trivial pursuits used to boost "I" into significance.

As a spiritual practice, mindfulness of breathing must be accompanied with respect to the five ethical guidelines; otherwise meditation is only mental gymnastics. Knowing this in meaningful terms is to sense it far down in our cellular life. The relativity and conditionality of our identity puts our ego into perspective. Insights into the ego reveal insights into all humanity. The Here-Now provides the raw material for understanding not only our "selves" but also other "selves." Being out of touch provides us with the raw material for fallaciously perpetuating our ego.

Contact with the respiration cuts off notions of being a particular type of person—always happy or depressed or angry. The view that "I am this type of person" has no continuity and belief in being any such label becomes a questionable habit. Other people, latent tendencies or both, stamp the habit of belief upon the kind of self we think we are. Preoccupation with "self" hinders the process of liberation. So direct awareness includes the changing nature of the breath and the self.

States of mind and structures of personality arise through contact. When contact ceases so does the compounding of the formation. Mindfulness of breathing, both formal and informal, serves to make change and impermanence abundantly clear. Not clinging to roles and identities safeguards us from fear of change, anxiety about the future and the cherishing of self existence. We can realize the Emptiness of assumed ongoing beliefs. One conscious inhalation, free from ideas about ourselves in that moment, cuts through the continuity of self identity.

Such forms of meditation humble egotism, revealing a wisdom about the conditioned nature of events and insight into the fluctuating character of phenomena. Mindfulness of breathing is more than a spiritual exercise for gaining some measure of calmness in agitated situations. It is a vehicle for eradicating selfish behaviour and suffering caused by grasping and clinging.

Awareness of the impermanence of all objects leaves little enthusiasm for possessive behaviour. Every "thing" and every "one" influence and give shape to every "thing" and every "one" else. Deep understanding of the interdependence of "things" and their lack of "self" nature is a feature of the spiritual life. It is in this spirit that the recognition of impermanence brings a willingness to abide free from clinging—even to the breath,

The moment that consciousness swivels its focus to another object, intentionally or otherwise, the old object is no longer present. Wisdom is full recognition of the impermanent character of objects and situations despite personal wishes. When objects become perceived as something substantial and inherently satisfactory we abide in a fool's paradise at the expense of wisdom and contentment. Clinging onto what has gone and pursuing fantasies is supping with the devil.

In spiritual realization, letting go is not an act of will but an organic response to realizing the Emptiness of being obsessed with people and objects. Seeing the absence of inherent existence and Emptiness of self exposes the joy of understanding. In spiritual awakening even teachers and teachings of liberation cease to be desirable objects of interest. This awakening embraces the breath, movements of mind and the Here and Now.

Meanwhile the breath comes and goes. Attention and objects dance along together in the rise and fall of conventional perceptions. In the wonder and mystery of the nature of things experience of impermanence does not expose the Ultimate Truth. A liberating wisdom does not prevent the everyday world from manifesting and passing from moment to moment. Our daily experiences reveal the mind inter-acting with senses and events.

Realization negates the belief that self and objects have real, inherent and enduring existence. Emancipation from the nightmarish grip of self-other obsession has no temporal-spatial reality since it knows neither characteristics nor location. There is no substance to existence and nonexistence when neither possess self importance. Fixed views of permanence and impermanence are a form of madness. The spell is over. We realize this profound

Emptiness that permits diversity of experience. The human organism responds with awe and wonder, and an undiminishing delight in the essential profundity of all phenomena. This vast revelation is Nirvana. Meanwhile inhalation and exhalation, experiences and events *appear* to come and go.

CHAPTER THREE

A MATTER OF LIFE
AND DEATH

When we were in our mother's womb we did not have access to seeing and hearing, smelling and tasting. It was reasonably quiet, safe and secure amid movement and stillness. The experience of waking up in the morning is not dissimilar from being born into the world. The breath, which may have been deep and silent, or rough and noisy in sleep, embarks on a different tempo upon waking. In the shifting of energy, the first intimation of a change of state is born. Organic life engages in an expanding surge; mindfulness is reborn at the sense doors. In the shifting of energy from one level to another, consciousness passes through the state of deep sleep and dream world to take birth in the conscious world again.

The sheer familiarity of the experience is hardly noticed as we stumble off to find tap water to stimulate us into yet another level of conscious being. As light of day strikes our eyeballs we begin to move; our yawns begin to diminish. Those first moments of day count for little whether we are determined to get on with the new day or are resistant to shaking off the slumber of the night.

We often consider the world of sleeping, breathing, waking up and putting water on our face as a rather banal activity instead of the very stuff of life. The way our day begins influences the rest of it. To trigger awareness and vitality we may need to remember that death is immensely long and our life is distinctly short. Yet, through our unwillingness to wake to the day, we live, act and have our being as though life was immensely long and death distinctly short.

In the stillness of the night an opportunity to understand the nature of existence arises that is denied in our involvement and obsession with our daily activities. In those moments of putting our head down at night we are in transition from the waking state, through the dream world, into deep sleep. Our consciousness of the senses begins to fade away—and, lo, the world is no longer present. The pleasures and pains of the day, dramas and comedies, successes and failures dissolve into the sublime silence of deep sleep. The night hours also offer time for quiet reflection on the processes of life.

Death and deep sleep seem to share similar features. We welcome deep sleep as an attractive lure from all the stuff of the day and yet we view death with concern and fear. We may endeavour to convince ourselves and others that we are not afraid to die, to become extinct to all we have known, loved and worked for. We cannot say how we will relate to our impending death. Hardly a soul has any idea at all where and when it will breathe its last.

When we die we would like to look back on our life as worthwhile or an extraordinary adventure which contained the fullest opportunity to abide expansively. We want that opportunity for ourselves, and, hopefully, for others too. Inner fulfilment is a matter of concern and unexamined ideas obscure a fulfilled life. We draw conclusions instead of realizing that we do not have to do anything special to discover a fulfilled life. Awareness, insight and heartfelt discoveries are the keys, not accomplishments and good fortune in the social sphere.

Sometimes we live as if life were eternal. We carry on regardless, ignoring the inevitable finiteness of our existence. At other times we are acutely conscious of the temporary character of personal existence. It may take the demise of a loved one, or a brush with our own mortality, or even something more subtle like a melting snowflake to alert us to our impending extinction.

Fascinated by what is novel, we quickly tire of it and look for something new, surrounding ourselves with various creature comforts. Such interest with temporal things keeps us from inquiring into the deeper issues of life and death. Sometimes it seems that nothing on Earth will disturb our fascination with the fashionable. Wisdom about death tempers the driving forces of the mind. Ultimately, what we get for ourselves amounts to nothing. If we lose our sense of purpose we might fall into a dismal state of despair, even destructiveness. Away from work, the endless hours spent shopping, cleaning and decorating provide us with a shallow sense of purpose. The mind must be kept busy and occupied even in leisure time otherwise we may start to think about things. Such thoughts may upset our constructed existence.

Our ritualistic daily habits inhibit awakening to an expansive vision accommodating life and death. Spiritually minded people do not display the same intensity of desire and abide with spiritual wisdom, good humour and cheerfulness amidst the fluctuations of daily realities. Even if we claim we are not afraid of dying and death we still cannot bear to lose a loved one, a possession or a pleasurable experience. We forget that the final breath ends all these. For those who remain deadly serious about life, death is often an utterly unwelcome event. There is little time for joyful and spontaneous activities; life is reduced to keeping the carpets and car pristine clean. The fall of autumn leaves is the whisper and reminder of personal circumstances.

We have settled for life's rewards almost exclusively materialistically or in a form of privilege. Failures, loss and funeral services intrude into the wish to uphold what we have gathered around us. The novel, the finite and the temporary handicap our potential for realization. The very prospect of death, either of ourselves or a loved one, churns our stomach sending our emotional and cellular life into apoplectic convulsions. Leaving this world is threatening, not only to life, but to all our efforts.

Diet, exercise and correct posture become the means to perpetuate our lives. We become determined to put off indefinitely the last day of our existence. Yet if we look into ourselves we may discover more vital reasons to look after our body, other than the wish to become an octogenarian or beyond. The apparent division between life and death is not as stark as we imagine. Concern with living a long life is a distraction from genuine realizations about the interrelatedness of life and death.

Thoughts about death leave us feeling very alone. Nobody can die for us. Having concentrated on our creature comforts we struggle to admit our age and our changing health. Discussion about death sounds morbid so some people cannot talk openly and honestly. Thoughts about the end of our life, or our bereavements remain private. This prevents exploration with others of the marriage of life and death—a marriage truly made for us all. We remind ourselves that when death is here we are not and when we are here death is not. Extinction appears like a menacing shadow, an enemy to be banished from our consciousness. There is a wisdom in penetrating into the Here and Now, birth and death, of our existence.

It is a blessing to be aware of the parameters of existence, to experience our mortality as an eternal tribute to life. Death serves the deepest interests of life by ridiculing our desires and self interest. Such profound revelations dissolve the divisions of presence and absence exposing simultaneously a vastness untouched by circumstances.

I never arrived
in time,
within this vast empty space
with landed dreams.

We conspire to hide death by isolating the dying, by immediately covering a corpse and by denying death's relevance to life. Faced with self negation, we treat death as a taboo, an alien state. Fear of extinction generates a bizarre relationship with the actual and inevitable ending of our existence as we have known it. We live as though the process of dying and death is a violation of our rights to continual self-determination. Success is controlling life and failure is loss of control. Every loss of a loved one becomes a sad reflection of our inability to be God and defy the laws of nature. We use every resource at our disposal to try to fight off the inevitable.

If we look deep inside ourselves we will find the strength to allow death to grace our home so that friends, relatives and neighbours can benefit from daily contact with a dying person, adult or child. Direct exposure to the process of dying and death of a close relative or friend can awaken our heart to the mysteries of life, particularly when we have laughed and cried with that person through the years. Home births and home deaths give us the opportunity to grow closer together. The last wishes of the dying hold more significance than the last rites.

Life's end is a breath away. Our selfishness and competitiveness seem madness when we realize we cannot take anything with us. In dispelling the taboo of death by bringing it out into the open we pay respect to life and express our love for the dying. Life and death are not enemies but complement the totality of existence.

We cannot be at ease with existence if we cling tenaciously

onto life, others and possessions. We are ready to say goodbye if we have looked the taboo of death in the face. Many children die more peacefully than adults because they do not cling to life. Within a generation we will be hardly a thought in anyone's mind. The unquestioning belief that the future is always available is a cosmic joke.

A young doctor was touring the wards of a large New York hospital. He exchanged pleasantries with the patients. During his rounds he arrived at one end of the hospital to visit a patient in a room on her own. The single room contained an iron lung that supported her existence and without which her lungs would collapse within a matter of minutes. A nurse handed the doctor the woman's chart. He smiled to the patient and began to read the information including her name, age, temperature and other facts. The chart reported her date of admission. She had been in the hospital for 30 years. The doctor shook his head with disbelief and then blurted out questions: "How do you stand it? You have been confined to this room all these years. Don't you get incredibly depressed?"

The woman looked at him and smiled. "No, doctor, not at all. Sometimes on a nice day a nurse opens the window behind me. The breeze comes through the window. It strokes my cheek. Those moments make it all worthwhile. Those moments reveal everything I need to know and everything I need to experience. I cannot ask for more." With a shake of the head, the doctor continued his rounds. He told me he would call in regularly at that single room to meet with the bedridden woman. She showed consistently a degree of warmth and happiness that evidently transcended her condition. She had unmasked the most ordinary and familiar. She had seen through the taboo of death. The original face of nature shone everywhere.

We do not have to regard funerals as the sad anthem of humanity. We do not have to experience mortality as the cruel end to all our efforts. Living daily in the face of a final departure concentrates our hearts and minds on the essentials of life. We hardly notice how our fear or obsession with death distorts our view of life. In trying to cope with our feelings of vulnerability, we seek to comfort ourselves by wishing to be immortal. We want the best of this world and the best of another world. The relationship to our own mortality induces wise or foolish living. To open our eyes early in the morning, to hear the sounds of the dawn chorus, to splash water on our face are all familiar. Yet would we be so apathetic to the new day, to the night hours, if we were facing the last week of our life? At some point, all these daily experiences will cease. In spiritual awakening life and death lose their marked distinction.

Scientific and religious communities perceive death in various ways. They present at least five viewpoints and we have possibly believed in one or more of them, wavered or never even thought about such matters and their significance in life.

A scientific view: We live once. We die once. Death is total extinction. This is rational. No proof of anything else is available.

A religious view: There is life after death. For those who find God, the Kingdom of Heaven is open for eternity. For those who reject God there is hell for eternity. The Earth is a brief home, a testing ground of our love for God.

A religious view: We are all waves on the ocean. Each wave is born and dies, repeatedly, according to the underlying forces. There is rebirth until enlightenment.

A religious view: There is reincarnation until the dissolution of the ego when the soul becomes one with the absolute.

A spiritualist view (nothing to do with spirituality): At death the "spirit" leaves the body and goes to another plane of existence. There is no extinction. The spirit may contact loved ones directly or through a medium or channel.

These beliefs offer some people a sense of certainty about the ending of the known. Others show indifference to the paradoxes of existence and get on with living their life as best they can. Yet death exposes itself daily in the cessation of a thought, ending of a relationship, an uprooted plant, the blast of gunfire and the lowering of a coffin.

We may think that our activities matter. Our sense of self importance carries more weight than heartfelt inquiry into the nature of things. The desire to be remembered as special distorts our actions; they become subservient to this desire. The dying of self is the dying of beliefs upon which the self gains its foundation. Our egotistical drives are meaningless despite the ironic disguise of meaningfulness. While lying in bed we can find out what waking up is. We can reflect on the totality of our existence when we put aside our day to day involvements that hide the mystery of all things. The melting snowflakes can touch the deepest place within our being.

Mortal frame,
dissolution of shape,
become ashes,
in a frosted field.

Perhaps when we rest at night we might regard going to sleep as dying: this *is* the end of life and no more tomorrow will emerge. The non-conscious world of sleep can serve as a catalyst for understanding the inseparable nature of life and death. Life knows completion with death while spiritual awakening brings fulfilment.

We devote our time to accumulating what we want with an implacable self righteousness. We think we know what is good for us; so our life becomes a capitulation to social and religious norms. Society's taboos remain unexplored; to step fully into life demands that we exorcise these superstitious beliefs. Our providence rests with our capacity to wake up. Realization is available every moment of our lives. We do not have to look further than the Here and Now to be enlightened.

Wisdom and a zest for life marks the flowering of our existence. A passion to understand the ordinary and everyday fills our being. Not subordinated to the demands of self or other, we experience enthusiasm for a liberated way of being. We celebrate the Here and Now rather than a wispy shimmer of it in the name of self-importance. Beyond the pursuit of self sensation, we become aware of the unfolding expansiveness of life. The middle of the night, when stillness is all around, is a useful time for reflection on these matters. Most people in our time zone are asleep and therefore at peace with each other. We so hate not to fall asleep because we don't wish to be tired the next day, but wakefulness in the night hours can inspire meditative reflections.

In her thoughts she convinced herself that she was too young to die. According to medical evidence she only had three months to live. She had worked in an office in the city, spent her holidays on hot Mediterranean beaches and had gone through a marriage and divorce. She was dying...slowly, virtually painlessly, but dying. The only sign was a slow but unmistakable loss of weight. One bitterly cold winter's morning she woke up. She tried and tried to get back to sleep. Shortly before dawn she wrapped herself in an abundance of woollen clothing. She took a deep breath, went outdoors and drove her car out of the garage and set off for the city centre.

She told me there was hardly a car on the road. "I just drove around and around. The atmosphere of the city seemed to share the same quiet atmosphere as my bedroom. As the new day came, the number of vehicles increased. People began emerging onto the streets. I parked the car on a main street and watched everything unfold—the nurses coming off night duty, the office cleaners going on duty, the occasional jogger, the lights turning on in apartment blocks, people walking quickly along the pavements, the homeless stirring on benches, the rumble of buses and delivery trucks.

"I came home shaken. I realized I had worked in the city for fifteen years and I had such a limited and prejudiced view of city life. Ever since that morning I have gone regularly to witness the new day. It seems to have taken the silence of the night to discover another face of the day. These days I drive into the city at dawn and then make my way to a coffee shop that opens really early. I drink a coffee and sometimes get into a conversation with the homeless, the night workers and the restless teenagers. We are all children of the night.

"For the first time in my life I feel alive. Such experiences make my illness worthwhile."

The dying woman has had to confront her mortality; awareness of her impending death has given her insights into life. She woke up on that cold winter's morning and responded directly to the situation. Most of the time we do not bother to be conscious of our mortality and the cessation of all the familiar. If we do, we might look at the night sky or touch a pebble on the beach with authentic awareness. We might experience a benediction that surpasses our worries or our rejection of death.

Still ocean, cool pebble,
twilight breeze.
I pass by.

CHAPTER FOUR

FRUITS OF OUR LABOUR

The concept of the city and the experience of attraction and aversion towards it are not separate events. The mind reveals the state of the city and the city reveals the state of mind. The city is a mirror for human existence for millions of people. City dwellers express many views about their city with its sights, sounds, smells and preponderance of information. They may describe it as an exciting or drab, filthy or clean, dangerous or safe place. Increasingly they speak about the levels of poverty and pollution. But city talk generates many words that say little and do less.

The air becomes almost tangible through the dark pollution that suffuses the atmosphere. The high-rise concrete matchboxes cast their shadows over the public. Cars, trucks and buses cram the streets—mobile containers with human occupants. Individuals sit alone behind their steering wheels heading for the office, shops and home. The pedestrians in the street scurry back and forth in the never ending task of trying to get things done. Tightly packed commuters are squashed in carriages of buses and underground trains, waiting to be squeezed out at each stop.

In offices, city planners try to find ways to make traffic move more quickly, to reduce the complaints of the travelling public. In the old days of horses and carriages they recall with nostalgia that the average speed of traffic in the city was 12 m.p.h. With the industrial age horses and carriages were squeezed off the streets to make way for cars that could go from 0–60 m.p.h. within a few seconds. Today city horses only perform ceremonial and police duties while the average speed of traffic in many cities is a breathtaking 10 m.p.h. Large, impersonal department stores and ever widening lanes of traffic have replaced narrow, winding lanes full of small family businesses, who knew the value of friendship.

Size, speed, efficiency and variety of goods are the hallmarks of progress as bland concrete architecture assaults the eyes and harsh noises harass the ears. The nose and mouth breathe in and out fumes. Coca-Cola, French fries and hamburgers are the order of the day. Pressures of time agitate the body. Time is money. There is little tolerance for those who cannot keep pace with the demands of the city. The elderly are driven off to geriatric ghettos.

Life becomes synonymous with pressure. Throughout the organized day, millions submit to the demands of telephones, bells and alarms with Pavlovian doglike regularity. Human beings become indistinguishable from each other, as stiff and organized as the computer screen emitting its demands to high rising careerists. Tied to such misfortune, the men and women of the suburbs arrive home at night exhausted and tense having endured the rush hour once again. In the bathroom, cleansing cream is applied to the face; the cotton wool turns from white to black as she or he rubs off the grime and squalid filth of the city. Civilization has insidiously invaded the pores of the skin, the eyes, ears and lungs, damaging delicate tissues ill-suited to such an environment.

Having slaved for hours everyday in upright plastic chairs, we arrive home to flop into over-priced, over-stuffed fashionable armchairs. The fruits of our labour! Escape from the invasion of city life is found in the home, whether the impoverished squat or palace of prosperity. We seek the comfort of an armchair and our room becomes a place of refuge, a sanctuary amidst a frantic existence. Through the acquisition of pleasure, we try to overcome the hard rigidity of daily life. The purchase of sensual experiences distracts us temporarily from the city treadmill. Television, a stiff drink, mild drugs, cinema and sport become forms of escape.

Millions are servants of the city machine. The pursuits of a minority, whose minds are addicted to power, profit and efficiency, have hijacked the destiny of individuals, businesses and perhaps the city itself. These men and women of the boardroom plot the next strategy to gain a greater share of the market. Seventy-five per cent of shareholders have never met members of the board, know nothing of the concerns of the managers and staff and have no contact with the victims of corporate decisions.

Shareholders have no real knowledge of the health and safety issues of workers or the impact of company policy on the environment, near or far.

The interest of shareholders is money. Money is all that matters. In some corporations, the board has decided that money grows on trees; therefore the holocaust of forests world wide. In the boardroom, use of resources, service to society and integrated livelihoods only merit interest through the campaigns of pressure groups. Shareholders, unconcerned with applied ethics, make a special contribution to creating a repulsive world.

The city masses, growing over the years, become like a lost generation without roots or foundations. Some have migrated from the impoverished countryside to the equally impoverished city to join the bright lights. They are like refugees often without a real friend, knowing only a handful of acquaintances. Major satisfactions are increasing the size of pay packets, shortening the number of working hours and lengthening holidays. The city is like a prison without walls and the summer vacation is the annual escape from this land of multiple bed-sits and high-rise flats.

The city appears dynamic compared with the slow pulse of rural villages. Yet, ironically, its appearance can be deceptive. From another perception the city appears like a slumbering beast unable to notice the suffering in its own streets let alone the suffering outside the city walls. However, this mass of humanity does begin to stir when prodded long enough and hard enough. An earthquake shatters the tenuous stability of city life in another country; high-rise apartments crumble like matchboxes crushing to death men, women and children. These apartments collapse owing to the poor safety standards housing developers have set. The housing developers had rushed through safety standards to maintain statistics for apartments built. City dwellers here then feel the danger of living in cramped conditions.

We reach out with cash and gifts. We try to find time to give financial support to those terrified and harmed by the hiccup in the stomach of the earth. Empathy with the suffering masses elsewhere enables us to transcend momentarily our senses dulled by our daily cycle. From the comfort of the armchair, we hear television news reports of the family trapped deep down in the rubble waiting to die. Friends and relatives on top of the rubble weep and wail in frenzied horror.

On another night television viewers watch the tragic effects of yet another famine, of tortured homelands without water and arable land. Families lie immobile on the barren earth lacking the strength to raise their arms for help. Again, we reach out to our cheque books offering gestures of relief for our vanquished brothers and sisters. Information from Africa's vast continent penetrates through the indifference and apathy of self existence. Gestures of kindness enable the ships and trucks to get under way bringing temporary relief to the thirsty, the hungry and the forgotten.

On another occasion news reaches us of the destruction of the tropical rain forests. Every few seconds, one species becomes extinct. In the Amazon huge fires rage to clear the rainforest. Short lived cattle farms replace lush vegetation, putting at risk the delicate balance of the ecosystem. Hamburgers are a few cents cheaper as a result. Again the public shifts its attention from the concerns of self to the campaigns to safeguard the ecosystem.

The city dweller dashes home through the cutting wind and cold rain. With not a thought for others, we fail to notice the tragedy of the homeless along the pavement, soaked and saddened by endless rejections. The place of rest for homeless people is the railway station, the park bench, the bus shelter, the odd night in the dosshouse and the cardboard box in the shop doorway.

"I am cold and hungry. Please give me small change for a meal." They beg for help, beg for eye contact, beg to be seen and heard. These untouchables wander the streets, orphans of our so-called civilization. Ignored by politicians, the business world and the public, they drift through each day in grim despair. Victims of insensitive values, they compete with the pigeons for a discarded lunch time sandwich, or search for scraps in the dustbins behind the fashionable restaurants. Occasionally we notice them huddled up in the cold on the steps leading to the underground. For a few moments self interest stops, we walk over to them and give a few coins, a warm smile and a few, supportive words. Despite isolation from each other in social terms there is contact, an expression of human warmth. The privileged and the underprivileged meet.

We feel genuine concern for destitute people. We observe the growing numbers of young people out begging, mothers with grime ridden children, the elderly shuffling along in oversized overcoats and alcoholics consuming a bottle of liquor in brown paper bags. We reflect for a few minutes on their plight and on the personal, social and political factors that have contributed to it. Then other thoughts begin to arise—thoughts imbued with self interest about yesterday, today and tomorrow. Having done our bit by offering small change, we rejoin the city in its sleepwalk. The possessed and the dispossessed go their different ways.

What would it take to stay awake, to keep the flame of generous spirit alight amidst the darkness of self centred existence? Self interest blinds us to the suffering and despair staring out from the eyes of these casualties who failed to join the rat race. They represent a momentary blip of our conscience—selfhood does not rule OK. But it becomes increasingly harder for the suffering to penetrate the world of the consumer.

In the shopping malls, countless items are for sale. They include CFC aerosols, mahogany wood, fur coats, E numbers, chemical food, paté de foie gras (liver of force-fed geese), contaminated fish, contaminated water, junk food, tobacco, alcohol, drugs, poisons, pornography, factory farm eggs, plastic bags, cruelty laden cosmetics, legs of chickens, backsides of cows, leaded petrol and so on. It is a shopping list of destruction. When we reach out for an item we need to recognize the interconnection of all things not just self-interest. Every item appears on the shelves owing to multiple conditions. Every item bought is the material expression of a value system where mindless purchasing masquerades as sanity. Yet the power of the purchaser is to say "NO" to that which harms and destroys.

Refusal to support destructive industries is a sign of love for life on Earth. Our choice of goods, no matter how brightly coloured, visibly displayed, neatly packaged and tastily presented, must come within the scope of global awareness. Awareness of the interconnection of things is a feature of spiritual awakening. Insights into the process of dependently arising goods challenges self gratification. Refusing to co-operate with the forces of harm also challenges the values of manufacturers and shareholders. We have the right to boycott what is unacceptable. The boycott is more than a political statement, a health conscious act or a reinforcement of personal values. To say "NO" to questionable products is an act of freedom, a statement of the anarchic spirit and a refusal to be brainwashed into accepting products considered vital for everyone.

Shopping bags laden with goods, we hurry on to the next appointment. We pick our nails, scratch our head and clench our jaw. The breath labours. Some travel to meet the lawyer wrestling to claim as much money as possible in a messy divorce case or insurance claim. Others meet the bank manager to secure yet another high interest loan to prop up a flagging business. Others have an appointment with the specialist for the results of medical tests. For others it is the perennial hunt for a better paid job with the eternal wait for a reply.

Amid all these concerns, the cry of those trapped beneath the rubble, the starving children, the tropical rain forests and the destitute city dwellers becomes fainter. Banishing compassion to the periphery of consciousness we ignore people, animals and environment; thus failing to ignite the spirit for change. Suffering humanity becomes lists of statistics. Warped by self interest and media that revel in disaster, we require bigger and bigger catastrophes to stimulate our responses to others.

We need to stop right in the middle of our existence as we rush between office chair and armchair to examine our priorities. With the mentality of a tortoise, we keep major issues at a safe distance by dwelling in the shell of self-existence. Yet we could focus our considerable intelligence on what really matters—the relief of suffering and the awakening of the human spirit.

This could act as a catalyst to transform consciousness and our way of being. We would walk the streets mindfully, sensitive to events in the immediate environment, boycott products that are destructive to people and planet, confront the ugly face of competition and exalt cooperation. It would mean change—an enthusiasm for vibrant, organic life, awakening out of insular selfishness into action born of compassion. This is the active exploration of the end of suffering.

By voicing our concern we touch the hearts of others. As we move with awareness through the city we emerge from the dark side of the monolithic concrete and mental fortresses. From this inner shift, we care for others with an assurance that we have nothing to worry about. By re-evaluating our role as city dweller, we can reflect on several of life's essential themes, such as ending suffering, serving others, and awakening. Quiet reflection helps us to unravel the patterns of inconsequential concerns so that we can make the deep issues of life our first priority.

If we grant ourselves permission to observe and change harsh realities, then happiness replaces despair, joy replaces fear and kindness replaces resentment. In the sublime interflow of the world of "YES" to people and planet and "NO" to marketed manipulation, we give only to receive. Our hearts are open to the mystery revealed amid the daily circumstances of phenomenal life. The awakening of spirit transforms our perceptions of city life. Despite the noise, the pollution, the mechanical routine and the oscillation between one kind of chair and another, we begin to feel the mysterious throb of city life as the vibrancy of human existence. Instead of hating the rush hour, we respond with wonder to the daily march of humanity going about its business. In spite of everything blatantly unsatisfactory about the city, we are committed wholeheartedly to the welfare of everyone, at home and abroad. At last we have broken through the drabness of our routine and discovered our precious contribution to the vast web of things.

CHAPTER FIVE

STEPPING OUT OF SHADOWS

We often blame politicians, the Establishment, the Church, modern life, the family or the individual for the ills of the individual or society. We use alcohol, crime, gambling, television and sex unconsciously to escape a soul-destroying existence.

Though we may engage in work that society commends, our life often confronts us with an eternal dilemma. We purchase our home, we marry and raise children and provide a range of material comforts only to find that our life feels empty. Our efforts to establish a secure base seem to flounder on the currents of unrest. We take out various insurance policies, eat the right food and exercise. Yet we are still vulnerable to germs and accidents.

We spend years at school employing our brains to become as highly qualified as possible. We want to secure a good position in life with a substantial salary, yet we feel the shadow of younger staff itching to move into our seat. In the areas where we have made the most effort to feel secure we experience the most insecurity. Fears of being under qualified, and in some cases over qualified, haunt us. Life seems unfair, unjust and unreasonable.

Insecurity permeates our behaviour, warning us of the danger of attempting to secure peace of mind through identification with loved ones, health and money. All too often these three areas matter more to us than anything else. As a result dependency issues harass our lives. We depend upon intimate friends believing that our friendship matters more to them than many other things. We depend upon personal, hereditary and environmental factors for our health. We depend upon our expertise, market forces and public interest for our money. We live in the shadow of our social world.

We are frequently blind to these codependent factors, foolishly believing that fortuitous circumstances are in our control. When we understand that there is no real security in social responsibilities, it does not mean that we neglect them. But we do not delude ourselves into thinking that life boils down to working hard to be secure. Once we let go of this conditioned idea we may experience an even greater degree of insecurity. But no joy exists if we spend our life either trying to make ourselves secure, or living in anxiety.

The proponents of security base their values on what is available in the conventional world. Possessions, loved ones, work, money, the need to belong and beliefs become the stage on which to live out fantasies and realize as many dreams as possible. All these efforts to be secure contribute to insecurity and existential terror. We are even willing to live in the shadow of another to feel safe.

It often means nothing to us to belong to Totality. Neglecting this sense of belonging sparks off emotional waves of identification with family, church, work or nation. Others overshadow us. Our sense of loyalty is then restricted to chauvinistic interests instead of to Truth, spiritual awakening and compassion. A small mind lives in a small world. We pay respect to ourselves and loved ones through a meditative and supportive vision, not through trying to be secure.

We imagine comfort is found within the limits of our immediate life. We live in a narrowly defined world based on narrow perceptions. The part—myself—wants to be somebody in comparison with other parts. By interacting with others, the part then gains character and distinction of its own. Repeating behavioural patterns cultivates an identity.

If we could shift our attention away from the part and meditate on Totality, the part might then fall into place. These meditations regularly practised would contribute to an expanded and insightful awareness of daily life. We could then reflect on our relationship to Totality and our interconnection with everything. Such meditations would influence our behavioural patterns, activities and conditioned views about different people, cultures and species. They might affect our regard for land, air, climate and water and our political views. Shifting to a perception of Totality would transform our feelings, thoughts and activities. We might discover the light of interconnection instead of living in the shadow of fear and insecurity.

For centuries western scientists have explored the nature of things by progressively breaking down objects into smaller and smaller particles. Scientists build huge, billion-dollar underground laboratories to attempt to smash subatomic particles into even smaller particles. Endless specialization is at the expense of awareness and realization of Totality. The preoccupation with the part, whether a subatomic particle, individual or nation, fails to consider the codependent factors that make up the part. The part exists because of the Totality. What surrounds the part makes it what it is.

The whole of humanity, the whole of life and the whole of the Earth are the concern of the wise. Tension arises when the parts are pitted against each other. Exaggeration of the place of the part disregards Totality. To see into myself, my relationships and my country does not mean rejecting them or dismissing the part as inconsequential. It means the part does not overshadow active awareness of Totality nor exist in conflict with it.

For example, we might consider the relationship with our children, towards whom we experience some of our deepest feelings. The child is a child of the Earth as much as "my child." If we only consider the child from a possessive position it is one part of life (the parents) holding control over the other part (our child). Parents and children belong to the family of life, to Totality, to the vastness of the nature of things. We also have the responsibility to ensure the Earth can support our children and our grandchildren. Understanding this, the part again is then seen in context of the whole.

Losing a child exposes the parent to the greatest grief. No other pain causes such religious doubts and despair. Fear of loss haunts parents, so anxiety levels around the children are high. Wisdom serves to protect children from exploitation, violence and ill-health; it becomes the raison d'être for the parent. Providing safety offers peace of mind to parent and child, a measure of security from the undesirable. Yet unending love cannot guarantee safety for the child. Circumstances sometimes cast away a precious and vulnerable life. Always relative, always conditional, always tied to the known and the unknown, the security we offer is provisional.

By opening up our awareness we experience our connection with all other parents: a woman went to see the Buddha carrying her dead child. The grief stricken mother begged him to bring the child back to life. The Buddha advised her to knock on every home in the village where she lived to ask if there was anyone who had not experienced the death of a loved one. She went from door to door but found that every household knew somebody who had died. In the immense fabric of life, birth and death become the strands linking us across our so-called divides.

When we realize the interdependence of existence we have no wish to force others to live in insecurity. We examine the forces inside and outside ourselves that affect the wellbeing of others and the environment. We influence each other in various ways. To be a whole person with an awareness of Totality we have to free ourselves from living subservient to another or having domination over another's life. When we examine our attitudes towards others we lose interest in exploiting them for personal gain. Love and compassion then enter personal, social and political life instead of being ignored.

Those who imagine they know best through a mistaken sense of superiority will expose others' vulnerabilities or harm them to get revenge. Those who bear grudges act unkindly. The intention behind this cruelty is to make others feel defensive and insecure. This persecution obscures the sense of Totality and a respectful and balanced relationship with others. The vicious mind erodes the welfare, security and happiness of others. When constantly threatened we lose confidence in ourselves and those close to us. We feel worthless and disheartened, thinking Truth and wisdom lie in the hands of others. As we lose trust in our perception, in ourselves and in the Totality of the situation we end up feeling beholden to those who dominate our life. But once everything is viewed together, concern emerges equally for all involved in the suffering of such behaviour. It is an act of courage to step out of the shadow of another, either as an individual or collectively. We need to examine our relationship to authority including how we express our own authority and how we respond to it in others.

We have a duty to listen and respond to the voice of those in anguish, who are low down in the pecking order. We have to hold accountable the manipulators of the vulnerable. We must understand that subjugating others to our beliefs and whims must stop.

Anything short of trying to end such domination over others, especially those with hardly a voice to speak out, is intolerable. Out of our deep sense of solidarity with each other we can act in wise and heartfelt ways to end the suffering caused by abusive human relationships. Realizing the end of conditions for suffering ends suffering. Together we have the capacity to explore the interconnected factors that make up the fabric of life. We recognize that others' actions affect us and we affect others. We know how abuse harms the welfare and security of us all. Our sense of Totality serves as a basis for thoughtful actions, and this spiritual awareness brings light to humanity.

Part Two
Relationship to the
Religious Life

CHAPTER SIX

GODS WITHOUT GODDESSES

Monks and nuns, priests and priestesses committed to a contemplative and caring life have an invaluable role to play in society. They are instruments for a depth of awareness and love. Those that express a simplicity of lifestyle and heart touching insights are servants of society. They deserve our respect and support regardless of their religion. Few people in lay life understand or appreciate the austerity and discipline that accompanies the lives of ordained contemplatives. We have much to learn from such women and men.

However, even in roles where there is a distinct absence of material privilege, there may be other forms of privilege at work. Today more and more ordained people are examining the divisions of privilege in religion and society. I wonder to what degree men are aware that many of their heart-numbing views, particularly towards women, are neither instinctive nor rooted in biological functions. They are learned responses, an unhealthy product of religious traditions that are identified with and acted out. By submitting to these unsatisfactory attitudes men deny themselves the opportunity for heart-warming and mutually enhancing communication with the other gender as well as with each other.

We justify these learned responses as systems of theology, psychology, biology and numerous other "ologies". Sophisticated discriminatory viewpoints are preached against women to uphold a male superior psychological stance, not for any actual value of the argument. This is particularly evident in the religious life where men's desire to maintain their roles and power can reach its zenith.

Male dominated social organizations survive through clinging to viewpoints which uphold a superior attitude towards approximately half the population whose physical appearance is slightly different from the other half. Physical differences are only relevant during sexual activity and trials of physical strength. Becoming deeply aware of the projections men put onto women, and women onto men, is the beginning of change. Men and women have engaged in a mutual conspiracy to maintain the status quo; men have mostly gained what they wanted and women have accepted subordinate roles. Having established this scenario for generations men are now obliged to re-evaluate their standpoints, their naive assumptions and their privileges. Men's claim to be stronger than women—they can throw a ball further, lift bigger weights and run distances in shorter times—seems to expand these limited physical considerations into all areas of life. Men in power still like to think men do things better.

Yet within this physical prowess, there are many exceptions, such as large men, elderly men, sick men. Men also do not share women's physical capacity to handle pregnancy and the pain of childbirth, or have to deal with hormonal changes, menstruation and round-the-clock breast-feeding. Setting aside biological considerations, differentiating between the genders seems purely arbitrary.

One significant area where men continue to uphold a dominant role is in the religious life around hierarchical structures and ordination. Men select and isolate certain religious roles and harness their interpretation of tradition to lend support to male supremacy. But it is not enough to perceive this passively; rather we need to change whatever circumstances reinforce the dogma of difference.

Vigilant investigation into the harm of promoting and identifying with gender differences beyond biological functions serves the interests of both genders. Through such insights it becomes untenable to exclude women from an equal role in the religious life. Roles, language, rituals, institutions and beliefs are all ready for critical examination and change.

The learning of conditioned responses occurs throughout adult life as well as in childhood. To assume there is any truth in our patronizing misperceptions is a superficial response to understanding human nature. For example, taking up the role of a priest or monk in the religious life may well include learning a set of responses that perpetuate the mythology of differences between the genders. In this way we are conspiring, unintentionally though it may be, to perpetuate the ideology of privilege. Only priests and monks in many religions can officiate religious services. They are the central figures in religious worship because they have the opportunity denied to women. Although men may regard themselves as supporters of women's issues, they must question whether male ordination, itself, perpetuates the continuity of women's subordination.

Women have some justification for regarding the religious hierarchy of men as hypocritical for supporting a men-only status while embracing the language of love, compassion and justice. The language of hypocrisy might seem rather harsh, but women may need to upset male religious orders until they hear the voice of women. Ordained men, who are resistant to change, must learn to take risks. For example, more and more devout women find it hard to attend Mass when every moment of the Mass denies women the opportunity to celebrate Mass. It is a turn-off for women to sing hymns and repeat prayers riddled with a one-sided "He" language. It can be hard to bow down before bishops, gurus, lamas, monks and mullahs sitting in elevated positions who would never dream of inviting women to share the same platform.

Continually having to experience a male privileged religion undermines for more women the experience of devotion and worship. Form and language reveal gender preferences so both genders assimilate discrimination as though there was inherent value in it. This reinforces the determination of women to explore further the movement for change. The religious life is just one illustration of the difference of opportunity based on gender; separate existences for men and women become fixed through language and roles.

When women have tired of calling into the darkness of men's hearts and minds they will no longer wait to be authorized or sanctioned through the male hierarchy. They will take the initiative for change themselves. The longer men hold back from inquiry into self and other, the quicker this change will come. Women who yearn for full participation in the religious life are beginning to realize that they don't have to wait for approval any longer. The movement towards change from learned responses is a movement mainly by women undertaken on behalf of both men and women. It is a clear illustration that personal salvation and the liberation of others are not two separate interests but interdependent.

The key to change lies in the often repeated religious injunction: others are to be treated as one wishes to be treated oneself. Letting that principle run deep into our heart influences conscious- ness to alter attitudes and behaviour. Kind and polite traditional views easily become a form of manipulation to sustain the myth of male superiority. Religious traditions have laid down as an article of faith the degree of accord given to men. Fear that a religious tradition will break down is often at the root of this; teachings of love challenge fear and prejudice. Men are afraid too that change means decline, deteriorating standards and disintegration of the religious traditions to which they dedicate their lives. The continuity of institutionalized views matters more than liberation and justice.

Men *seem* to possess vast amounts of power. Like any other object of inquiry, power is empty of any inherent existence, any independent reality. It requires the cooperation and support of other people. Through resistance or passivity power gains credibility. Women must also take responsibility for this unsatisfactory situation in the religious life. Thoughtful women are making great efforts to get orthodox religious men to reconsider their view of women. In a bizarre way, this struggle reinforces the notion that such men do possess power. This struggle for equality will continue since women transfer power to men by acknowledging their position.

Not surprisingly women faced with men's tactics of using old religious texts in any religion to support their views find themselves in a considerable dilemma. Do women stay with the "powers that be"? By trying to persuade men to change, they reinforce the belief that men hold power. The more intractable men are, the more likely women will call it a day. Instead of waiting around for men to come out of their tortoise-like position and give women the acknowledgment and equality they seek, women are taking power into their own hands. They are exploring alternative forms of the spiritual life, taking ordination, instigating new myths or resurrecting old myths respectful to female language, rituals, roles and forms. The intractable position of the male ushers in that of the female. A "She" language replaces the "He" language of the religion. The waltz goes on.

Away from the religious life men often have their own way and this affects how they relate—be it to a foetus, a partner, wild animals, tropical rain forests or the Earth. For example, in a traditional nuclear family, the wife or partner has responsibility for the widespread and never ending task of maintaining a home. At the end of the man's working day the moneymaker returns home, sits at the head of the table, with full expectation for the evening meal to be placed in front of him. Sitting there, the "breadwinner", the father, the husband surveys *his* household—the dutiful wife, the obedient children and the possessions that *he* has worked for.

This scenario repeats itself throughout many societies. Not surprisingly, half of western marriages and relationships end in divorce and a significant factor is men's inability to notice how their wives are feeling day by day. Men tend to ignore or dismiss the daily experiences of their partner or wife. Even when men ask, they communicate a subliminal message that they are not really interested. Men are often more interested in the weather report, watching football on television or having a snooze on the sofa. Traditional men treat their wives as another commodity in the home who ought to function effectively day in and out. They think that because they provide their partners with a new dress or latest consumer gadgets "the woman" has nothing to complain about. Women are not blind to this form of treatment, so it is not surprising when researchers tell us that women in the West today end seven out of ten failed relationships.

Many women work for an integrated and intimate relationship founded in respect. They strive towards equal opportunity and cooperation in the home as well as the churches, synagogues, mosques and temples. But a time comes when there is no point in continuing any further. Male blindness, the unwillingness to listen, prolongs the polarity of men and women. Many women have decided they deserve something better. They are telling men they can sit at the head of an empty table! Often men fondly imagine they are not like other men. "I wash up after all!" Washing up after dinner by the male is not a sign of his understanding equality in the home, it is nothing more than a normal household duty. (Washing up takes little time compared to preparing a meal).

Family men or office managers are frequently not used to listening. They want to stamp their authority on the situation, get things back under control and stop their partner hassling them, children or staff. This attitude is a prescription for ending marriages, confusion for children and resignations at work. Male attitudes work in a similar way in religion. Men who cling to authority, rigid tradition and texts tend to feel that "militant feminists unnecessarily hassled them," as one priest said. He claimed that women seeking equality were an "unrepresentative group of women." Orthodox religions have become nostalgic about the time when there was unspoken agreement about the patterns of domination and submission.

Men like to exert their influence in other ways. By manipulating circumstances to their advantage, they like to make physical contact with women This can be in the form of an innuendo, a brushing of the body, or abusive language. This form of behaviour even occurs during the middle of a meaningful discussion on gender relationships. Women regard such displays of arrogance or inappropriate physical contact as offensive and disconnected from meaningful communication. The distorted perception that regards woman as object influences men's ability to show true affection, love and sensitivity, and men are often not aware of the impact their behaviour has on women. Communication may include a friendly touch, which most people generally welcome, but an unwelcome touch from a man to a woman, and less commonly from a woman to a man, is repulsive.

The business world uses physical intimacy between men and women to sell products. Symbols of genitals are found in advertisements. Societal judgments and personal experiences often result in perceptions of women and men as sex objects. Men enter denial when such sexist behaviour is pointed out. They may claim they were simply affectionate and it was not a "come-on." Upon meeting a woman men often focus upon some physical aspect—her breasts, her backside, her legs, her lips. In doing so they reveal a conditioned mind and an inability to recognize the difference between beauty and lust. Similarly some women ogle men and sensitive men find this very unsatisfactory. Sometimes women ogle men to get revenge; they adopt a male way of behaving and this promotes a manipulative circle of behaviour. Women who collude in notions of male supremacy whether in the home, church or society are as responsible as men for maintaining this unsatisfactory state of affairs. Making significant changes in behaviour can be just as difficult for those who tend to be submissive as for those who feel superior.

Physical contact from a man to a woman during conversation is appropriate when there is trust and true affection, free from manipulative overtones. Touch and the way men use their eyes reveal their state of mind but also the way men think about women communicates itself whether they are aware of it or not. Men imagine that the secret corners of their fantasy life remain well hidden. They come to regard the conquest of women as natural and normal when they see other men behaving in a similar way. In some respects gay men who are respectful and supportive of women can serve as something of a model for heterosexual men. By not needing sexual involvement with women, friendly gay men are able to relate from a different perspective, a perspective not charged with innuendoes and tones of manipulation. More important than certain types of men as models for appropriate behaviour is the ability to communicate respectfully to others.

It becomes increasingly more difficult to choose celibacy in the religious life in a society obsessed with sex. Ordained celibates often use personal control and will power to prevent the release of sexual energies. This repressive pattern then expands itself into control over the tradition, the interpretation of religious texts and the clinging to authority. Gods *need* to rule and control without the shared presence of goddesses. Repressed patterns have their roots in clinging to standpoints, unresolved patterns of hostility and the emotional need to feel on top of a situation. Religious texts often rationalize these patterns, but liberating ourselves from the prison of conditioned perceptions requires insight and understanding into habitual behaviour.

For example, a man may see out of the corner of his eye a woman whom he perceives as attractive. This experience can become the basis to ogle her as an object. Projections of desire distort the appearance of the woman and the subsequent feelings, thoughts, speech and behaviour then impact on the way of relating to her. Men sometimes imagine that their desires will be fulfilled through the actualization of fantasy. The compensation for feelings of inadequacy in a man's life is often control over a woman. He imagines that keeping the presence of a woman, or conquest of her will give him a sense of self-worth. What men get from conquest is a temporary relief from the need for attention. The capacity to acknowledge the consequences of male attitudes to women is a sign of a growing maturity in interpersonal relationships. In the religious life this means looking into the desire to control, the way men and women use their sexual energies, cling to traditional standpoints and accept positions.

The inability to respond to the endless appeals for equal opportunity reveals more about personality structure than it does about religious texts. We realize the absurdity of treating each other with negativity. To make changes for equality and justice is an authentic expression of the spiritual life. The surrendering of biased belief systems challenges men and women right down to their genitals—a foundation for some of the most unsatisfactory ideas between the sexes.

It is in this spirit of emancipation for men and women that the capacity for dignity becomes apparent. Shared roles between genders belongs to the process of spiritual awakening of individuals, couples and institutions. Love, trust and respect are essential values of the spiritual life. Those qualities bring out similar qualities in others. Religion gains a fresh significance and members uplift each other through trust and genuine affection.

The history of male privileges in the religious life is self-evident and long standing. The time has come for a liberating renaissance. The joy and harmony of shared roles and language will awaken a new generation of women and men who wish to participate in a nondivisive expression of spirituality. Faith is a cornerstone for the meaningful change of religious institutions. Faith can move mountains, even mountains of unreasonable theology that support Gods without Goddesses. In enlightenment there are neither men nor women.

CHAPTER SEVEN

THE TEACHER, TRADITION AND BOOK

Society produces two types of spiritual people. One identifies with orthodoxy and the perpetuation of what seems safe and secure. The second is a seeker. Not content with the various orthodox religious institutions, the seeker explores alternatives. Upon finding and experiencing something meaningful, the traditionalist and the seeker are willing to devote time to those who have had similar experiences.

The traditionalists often embrace the religion of their birth, the predominant religion of their society or peer group. This may be from conviction or from the wish to stay with what is comfortable. Reverence often is not developed toward other spiritual teachings; they may even be subjected to ridicule. Identification with services, prayers, rituals and language fossilize the chosen religion; faith becomes rooted in the forms of the religion. Services of other faiths, even of sects within the same religion, appear suspicious or incredible.

Fixed in time, religious beliefs become resistant to change and re-evaluation. They then have a hold over consciousness, actively hindering genuine spiritual development. Perhaps, more than many other forms of attachment, dogmatic religious beliefs succeed in deterring people from authentic spiritual expression. The dramatic decline in church attendance, as well as the loss of faith in dogma, show the gradual loss of hold any religion has over people today.

Yet various religions fail to recognize the relationship between dogma and decline in the numbers of active members. As the

Church grew, it exercised increasing control over people's lives. It identified with the State and began to conform to political will. This union of church and state developed at the expense of spiritual awakening. One obvious example is the choice between "love thy neighbour" and making war for "Queen and Country". The latter clearly takes priority in many cases with the church conducting victory services. Church and State share an unholy marriage.

The history of state religion exposes constant attempts to thwart genuine spiritual expression and is largely useless in offering spiritual direction. It does little more than conduct a handful of services from birth to death. But this decline of faith in established religious forms has not changed the need for deep spiritual transforming experiences and their application in the world.

Unlike traditional religion, authentic spiritual teachings have no interest in converting anybody to any "ism." Spiritual wisdom questions such motives.

A believer's adherence to a particular religion or sect may stimulate a variety of perceptions. Most noticeable is how the convert views those who see things differently. Before any religious experience the believer may not hold strong views about other faiths, but the time often comes when he or she begins to identify intensely with one set of beliefs. This may lead to the formation of a strident set of views reinforcing intolerant and aggressive tendencies. The differing beliefs of others then appear threatening so the converts must condemn them. This in turn strengthens the tendency to cling to her or his own religious experiences and their interpretation.

Conformity and surrender to fixed doctrines, which appeal to some, deter others. Can the spiritual life be free from following a tradition or enlightened being, alive or dead? The Great Book, The Great Teacher and the Great Tradition can distract seekers from meaningful realizations, achievable in a simple, unattached spiritual life. We may describe ourselves as members of a particular religion, but this association may exist unexamined. Our religion may make hardly any difference to our daily life. We make the occasional prayer at a time of crisis or infrequently attend services. Breaking away from such tenuous religious ties is of little consequence in pursuit of spiritual truths.

The capacity to reduce the truths of spiritual life to a matter of convenience is not unfamiliar in religion and is the despair of those who make compassionate sacrifices in the name of their beliefs. The minister, dedicated to the welfare of the members of the church, sees how few are willing to make sacrifices to find Truth. He sees that all too frequently he merely welcomes the newborn, blesses the dead and conducts rituals. The minister, too, may have lost his spirit. Religion has become a mild appendage to the rest of existence.

The priority of personal, family and social ambitions marginalizes spiritual development. If religious life is a prop to help deal with some temporary anxieties the honourable thing is to renounce all ties with religion, as most do anyway. The current spiritual malaise curses all. Views as believer or disbeliever need to be cast aside to pursue the Truth. To be born again is restarting in a state of unknowing, committed to spiritual awakening. Unimpressed with the certainty of the convictions of others, the seeker travels deeply into awareness, inquiry and silence.

Cutting through the superficialities of secular existence, the seeker may soon discover that it is unnerving to enter the unknown. Religious sharks roam the deep ready to drag the luckless diver into the dark. Entering new territories of consciousness, one is vulnerable to powerfully persuasive charismatic figures. In the name of enlightenment, some so-called spiritual masters express pathological states of mind. The seeker has to listen attentively and respectfully to his or her own inner experience, and be watchful of the need to reach out and grasp. Yet, at the same time, the seeker needs to abide with a warm and expansive heart responding to the spiritual values and insights revealed around her or him.

The seeker thus takes risks through diving into spiritual exploration. Since the deep is unknown and unexplored, wise spiritual friends and spiritual practices become useful tools. Contact with like-minded people in the spiritual life is indispensable. It is no easy undertaking to explore spiritual practices without becoming swallowed up in them. Thinking ourselves ignorant in spiritual matters we are likely to hand over all authority to others who regard themselves as more developed along the path. Cults, sects and ideologies haunt society, collecting the vulnerable, the suffering, the intelligent and the successful. Using a variety of mind-bending inducements and emotional hits, described in religious language, religious leaders build up their empires.

Some seekers, who revert to their native religion, may seek spiritual guidance in a familiar religious language and doctrine. They can discriminate wisely between unsatisfactory dogmas and teachings of love and compassion. Others avoid a new faith and avoid returning to the faith of their childhood. They prefer to rely upon themselves for spiritual wisdom. But in rejecting all outer teachings, they may cling to the notion of spirituality as being personal. Such understanding may have many shortcomings and be merely a way to hide behind an untested personal doctrine. Others choose to explore the expanse of spiritual teachings without restricting themselves.

Spiritual wisdom is not unconditional surrender, as some religious leaders would have us believe. It is the ability to go into a movement or group with our eyes wide open to the various devices employed to manipulate consciousness. The methods used to convert the mind to consumer values or religious values are remarkably similar; a common denominator is persuasion.

For some people one particular religious experience may seem sufficient for a life long conversion. They do not realize that attachment to such an experience contributes to the ills of individuals and society. Such rigid views breed animosity and conflict while a healthy society encompasses a range of beliefs and a diversity of perceptions. Seekers who claim to have found the Truth easily become smug or intense. Claimants' lives become subordinate to this conviction, supplanting humility, generosity of spirit and the joy of unknowing. Their Truth is expressed as arrogance and unresolved personality issues.

Healthy communication with other seekers requires diligence to protect consciousness from gross or subtle indoctrination. It is hard to be honest and question, easy to cave in to pressure, persuasion and conformity with others. Believers are prone to accusing seekers of pride, holding back and fear of letting go. Such accusations strike a chord with the seeker, who is unconsciously reminded of past times when he or she held back through fear from involvement. However, sometimes these defences arise from wisdom and are a healthy response.

The inner voice of wisdom does not conform to group pressure, but when suppressed the seeker may undergo later an emotional release—a sudden conversion. After this has subsided the seeker is likely to experience immense peace as well as deference to the leader, the book, the tradition and the group, or all four. The seeker may sacrifice authentic liberation—the jewel originally sought—through identification with persuasive people, whether adherents number hundreds or millions is irrelevant. Can there be letting go, emotional releases, ecstatic spiritual experiences without blind conformity to the aims and beliefs of the leader or the group? What does it mean to be deeply spiritual *and* keep our eyes open? What does it mean to be receptive and not naive? If there are inner doubts, then it helps to take a breathing space away from the voices of influence.

A Teacher, Tradition or Book often prescribes a format for living. Violation shows failure of commitment and understanding. Believers feel guilty for failing to conform; followers accuse them of disrespect to the authority, who knows the Truth, but a leader's arrogance can obscure the Truth. We wonder how someone can limit his or her Freedom by identifying tenaciously with a belief structure: liberation surely must include release from such adherence. But followers prefer living with the known, namely The Teacher, The Book or The Tradition and the Tribe rather than facing the transforming intensity of silence and the unfathomable unknown. Becoming more involved in belief structures, they lose interest in family, old friends, work and creativity. But they tell others how much love and commitment they have and of their willingness to give up everything for the cause.

As time goes by, believers adopt the biases and prejudices of the group. They imitate the mannerisms of the living authority; incessantly mention his or her name. They copy the tone and style of language of the authority. Believers are obedient to the dictates of the leader whose opinions are treated as Truth. The personal items the authority figure uses become objects of awe. A tiny circle of intimates protects him or her from the negative vibrations of outsiders supposedly blinded by ignorance. Believers treat those who leave with disdain or make defamatory statements about them. They display an inability to admit that the departure of followers may be an expression of an independent and mature attitude.

Intense believers lose active concern with the suffering in the world and the work for peace and justice—unless it contributes to building up numbers of members. Love for the world becomes conditional on finding converts. They cannot see further than the group's beliefs—an enclosed Truth restricts consciousness rather than liberates it. Believers speak positively of the significance of religious commitment and its impact upon their personal life, but they may fail to comprehend why others are not interested in the same fate! People in the group may spend much time discussing, writing and telephoning friends and strangers, or even knocking on front doors, to persuade others to be involved.

Doubts and negative reactions among members, especially when directed towards the founding source, are not tolerated. Fear of rejection deters believers from openly voicing dissent. The original quest for Truth, liberation and awakening erodes. Or worse, there is a claim to have found the Truth, which must be organized, promoted or formed into a marketable product. Once involved hard-core believers become unable to question the psychological and emotional reasoning behind their commitments. If the questioning is unable to take place inwardly, what hope is there for open debate to take place outwardly? What hope is there for a genuine realization free from the overshadowing influence of another or others? Questioning, with or without fear, is the seed of liberation, the murmuring of Truth.

The breeding ground for cults often lies deep within the psyche. Unresolved feelings of dissatisfaction and insecurity reverberate so the only wish is to belong to the belief system. The recognition that we already belong to the immensity of things expressed as the Here-Now is tragically ignored. No beliefs or practices make a difference to the Ultimate Truth. Cult members express strong convictions, self-confidence and personal satisfaction. They may well appear to be happy—something possibly they have never experienced before. But the happiness is *within* the framework of the conviction, the authority and the companionship. Spiritual awakening is discovering a liberating happiness not dependent upon such structures.

A happiness confined within spiritual structures reveals that all is not well. The dependency and need for contact with the leader may bring forth from the follower enthusiasm, excitement and devotion. But these sensations may have nothing to do with wisdom and liberation. The believer will have to make up his or her mind about the need to hold such beliefs. Deep down, the believer may simply want feelings of security and companionship. The group may provide this and so the believer is happier in the group than outside it. But the group may not offer a spiritual awakening genuinely free from clinging to beliefs and narrow views.

Believers often like to remember the time of initial contact with their chosen path. They report that they were searching for something meaningful or they believed that their friends who joined a sect had found something. Others report that they were not seekers but the authority revealed something was missing from their lives. It is understandable that people should wish to share their personal experiences of conversion with others, but all too often the motive is to persuade the unconverted that the believer has "got something" the nonbeliever hasn't. Identification with The Teacher, Tradition and Book closes the doors of emancipation, and loyalty eventually replaces significant spiritual experiences. The believer does not have the assurance to evolve out of this restricted condition and so remains in a state of submission. Believing exclusively in the words of the teacher is like entering a dark tunnel with no light at the end.

Nonbelievers often display similar attitudes to believers. They claim that they alone are living in the real world. They exhibit the same kind of dogmatic adherence to their views as believers do and condemn them as out of touch with reality. Many nonbelievers are not aware of their adherence to the cult of cynicism or the cult of consumerism. They imagine that the real world consists of producing and consuming goods, obsession with money, striving to be successful and watching television most nights of the week. Nonbelievers frequently show a disdain for all religious experiences and the subsequent sense of peace. Believers and nonbelievers have much in common.

Cynics like to ridicule people in religious groups. They fail to consider how personal and social pressures may have acted on believers. One attraction of becoming a follower is counteracting the sheer monotony tied up with daily existence. The life of the consumer is empty of depth. Work, unemployment, study, food, sleep, pleasure and pain all leave a vacuum that no amount of activity or success can fill.

For some the price for Freedom is a constant and vigilant mindfulness not to identify with narrow or selfish beliefs. Continual mindfulness requires the quiet determination to speak out when unsatisfactory situations occur within religious groups. The seeker forms a relationship with a particular teacher, but this voice of authority has no existence outside this relationship. Yet these forms of spiritual authority can be invaluable for the seeker to gain depth of experience, insight and revelation that transcends these forms and relinquishes dependency upon them. Devotees to the spiritual life must hold their authorities accountable otherwise critical perceptions are left in the hands of the cynics.

The wish to have access to spiritual teachings necessitates a commitment to discernment. The ability to discern safeguards those committed to the spiritual life from going overboard or drowning in lavish praise of a teacher or teachings. Those who listen to spiritual teachings confirm the teacher. The one who offers the teachings confirms the listeners. Thus it is the devotee who makes the teacher substantial. The voices of authority and the ears of the devotees are codependent but this codependent truth is not understood. Followers acknowledge the teacher, but forget their own part in a codependent situation. Elevation of the teacher is at the expense of an understanding of codependency. Teachers only have existence through the listeners' presence!

This awareness serves to protect the heart from the naiveté of becoming beholden to another in the disguise of spiritual surrender. We do not serve love, justice or Truth by becoming enmeshed with gods or teachers—with the corresponding neglect of understanding codependency. The affirmation of self, either of another or ourselves, perpetuates a blind spot that only clears through direct insight into the nature of things. Believers exploit this blindness; they claim fulfilment while others are deluded. The conviction something is missing makes seekers vulnerable to persuasive voices. The challenge is not to become beholden to anyone anywhere, grossly or subtly. The realization of joyful liberation is close. Enlightenment dissolves the relative truth of the teacher, the teachings and the faithful.

CHAPTER EIGHT

THE NARROW HEART

The entire range of religious books, past and present, is as much a hindrance to spiritual enlightenment as an asset. Their endless repetition of particular words and themes forms the structure of religious beliefs. Out of this wide range the believer is likely to use a small group of words to form a personal belief. Deleting certain words from a religious vocabulary would enable different faiths to find a common ground of agreement.

This book is not apart from its reader: the reader's perceptions determine the meaning of this book. It has neither meaning nor ultimate existence of itself. What you think of the book is what you think of it. Please be mindful whether you think much of it, little of it, something of it or nothing of it. Its appearance as a book occurs in the moment of contact and ends at the end of contact and the passing of the reader's thoughts about it.

The unwillingness to examine the way religious words—God, Truth, sin, karma, grace—are employed empowers language. The belief that words describe "realities" reveals assumptions. Based on these premises, the world takes shape with variations of truth and reality composed of a range of physical, mental, spiritual and metaphysical descriptions. Ultimately, words cannot describe anything. Language is as much a mystery as the universe it seeks to describe.

Words appear to mean something when linked with other words to form a conceptual system. Persuasive and passionate repetition of key words does not make them the Truth. Blind convictions sound more and more abstract for any person spiritually grounded. Using a string of words to form conceptual structures has a useful part to play in the conventional world. But we cannot expect people from other cultures to understand our religious terminology when religious terms baffle people in our own culture. To believe ultimately that a conceptual system stands for something is more an amusing thought than a self-evident fact. Whatever is expressed is without essence.

We form views long before we hear anything which challenges them. We know our position, expect to defend it and attack opposing positions. We believe vehemently in our views, and not doing so implies indecision. We do not want to admit we have changed our mind, superficially or deeply, because we might lose face. The image of being consistent, strong and forthright may matter more to us than we realize; the string of words may matter far less. Perhaps we adapt our garlands of truth to the image we want to present to the world. At times, we may have to explain to others why we are saying one thing today when we said something quite different previously. The call to be consistent doesn't seem to make allowances for change, for error, for the admission of mistakes. We want to appear infallible or conversely, to make a virtue of appearing contradictory.

We conspire to keep a statutory view of the way things are through language. It is not just a matter of examining the nouns and verbs we employ to reinforce our beliefs in a static situation but also the prepositions. For example:

"I am in this religion."
"I am in this practice."
"I am in this relationship."
"I am in this position."
"I am involved in this exploration."
"I am looking into myself."
"I am into meditation."
"I am in touch with God."

The concept "in" enters many areas of interest that preoccupy our mind. Not noticing the use of this word, we ignore the convictions linked with "in" or "out." The mind easily becomes bogged down in involvement with one or the other. Much happiness and unhappiness occur around the notion of being "in" something or "out" of something. Throughout our lives it matters whether we are "in" or "out" of a relationship, a job, or money. Rather than question our assumptions about "in" and "out" we hold to our views despite the associated pleasure, fears and pains. We beat ourselves up through defining ourselves in these terms becoming obsessed about one position or the other. We believe in the inherent value of one over the other.

The craving to be "in" something and the strategies used to accomplish it contain fear of the opposite. Rather than examine their interconnection, we perceive the two positions as entirely separate entities, even in competition with each other. We believe that "in" or "out" makes a world of difference, that reality is black and white. We can search for examples of where "in" and "out" do matter, do make a real difference such as, in life and death. The patient in intensive care, the worker suddenly made redundant or the prisoner waiting for parole will dwell daily on the significance of the differences between "in" and "out." These examples touch our concern for human existence. But even here we need to examine how we view the situation, especially if it appears all doom and gloom. What value and dependency are placed on "in" or "out"! Life then becomes reduced to imagining that this is all that matters.

"In" and "out" are key concepts in thinking and imagining about events. This also happens in the spiritual life; we build up a frame of reference for behaviour. Categories affirm the spiritual life and another set says what runs contrary to it.

Spirituality requires a tremendous amount of dedication. It is not an easy undertaking to enlighten heart and mind. Sacrifice and letting go of selfishness are vital factors in developing spiritual awareness. The function of spiritual teachings is to offer direction, highlight the value and dangers of the spiritual path and point out liberation.

The cult is a danger to spiritual awareness. A central characteristic of a cult is its aura of exclusivity. A cult exhibits addiction to the presence of and surrender to the leader. Cults may pass through several phases, but each phase has credibility at the time. Since members of the group may pass through different phases at different times it is frequently not possible for followers to understand each other. The cult regards devotion to the leader and the cause as commitment to Truth, enlightenment or God. Those with strong convictions treat with suspicion those who are critical, wavering or passing into the final stage. They regard them as deviants who have fallen by the wayside.

The first phase is exposure to various spiritual experiences. The leader is granted central authority. Cult members come to believe in the historical significance of the leader, and that the Truth lies exclusively through this person. Regarded as enlightened, one with God or a prophet, the leader is a source of refuge.

The second phase is pursuing contact with the leader and followers. Being with the leader is blissful. Followers will discuss among themselves with awe and admiration the qualities of the leader.

The third phase shows the cult becoming like a family; closely knit, with conversations focused around personal experiences of contact with the leader. Followers refuse to engage in keen exploration of other spiritual practices. Leader and followers do not tolerate doubts, and the demand upon the individual is total commitment.

The fourth phase is dealing with whispers of dissatisfaction occurring among some followers. Voices from outside the cult and a small minority from within raise difficult questions. The leader's behaviour, including abuse of power, sex, money or obsessive arrogance disturbs certain followers. The leader and majority of followers order out those who express doubts or find some pretext for their exclusion.

The fifth phase is disillusionment. After weeks, months or years, the leader's promises of enlightenment or salvation, and the repetition of claims, begin to sound monotonous. Devotees show disenchantment.

The sixth phase is a growing awareness of the outside world and the possibility for a meaningful spiritual existence outside the influence of the cult. This is often a distraught period and much unhappiness or depression can emerge following loss of identification with the leader and the followers. The leader loses his or her power of control and charisma as the projections diminish.

The seventh phase is a period of change. There is a greater capacity to make one's own decisions and take responsibility for them. Reflecting on his or her relationship to the cult, the follower acknowledges past phases of hero worship, narrowness of heart and emotional dependency. Authentic spiritual experiences and insights are identified. There is a greater sense of freedom and relief at being out of the cult's shadow.

Not all those identified with a cult will pass through the final three phases. There is no choice for those with emotional addiction; it matters a great deal to remain "in" the belief structure. To be thrown out may be devastating and bring intense feelings of lack of self worth. Mesmerized by power and projected spiritual authority, the cult tolerates arrogance and bullying from the leader. Expelling a follower renews the sense of self worth of the remaining cult members. They believe they are among the chosen ones, who are truly committed. The cult may also take the leader's decision to expel a follower as proof of his or her nonattachment to building up numbers. It is common for cult leaders to condemn cults.

Some people leave voluntarily and some do not. Both may experience feelings of disillusionment. To some the world seems an even more disillusioning place to abide in, so they return. They are addicted to the group experience. Humbly and apologetically, they confess that their ego had got in the way. They return with devotion and gifts. The followers then hear the teacher readmit those who are repentant back into the fold. They feel joy at the "compassion" of the teacher. The rebellious disciple has learnt his or her lesson and will never question the teacher's authority again. There is restoration of order. Control is back in the hands of the teacher and contentment suffuses the hearts and minds of the followers.

This scenario repeats itself among the countless sects, cults and religious organizations around the world. Obedience has frequently mattered more than wisdom and freedom. And, without being too simplistic we might say that what matters is the feeling of "being in" rather than "being out." The follower wants to get something from the commitment. It is assumed that initial benefits will lead to greater spiritual gains. The follower can't imagine that the same experience is available elsewhere. Hating to be cut off from the intimacy of the group the follower behaves in a submissive way.

Concern and questions arising in the mind of the sincere seeker often include:

"Why do I have no choice when it comes to making a commitment? Do I undervalue myself? I feel spiritually aimless."

"I want to find something that my deeper spiritual feelings will respond to wholeheartedly. Others in the group seem so loving towards each other, so committed, that I find it attractive and magnetic. I want to be like them.

"What would it mean to abandon the idea of being a follower, to let go of the idea of being like them and face the bareness of no quick answers to the deeper questions of existence? It might mean a re-evaluation of who I am and what I am committed to.

"What is a healthy attitude towards others involved in a cult? What is a healthy attitude towards leaders?"

Freedom includes the right to express concerns, to speak out when the leader dismisses, abuses or undermines individuals. Expression of concerns safeguards followers from emotional addiction: when followers condemn me for criticizing the tenets or the teacher, then I will know that these are not the people to be involved with. I understand that those who display flashes of anger towards authority figures may be making a valid point needing to be heard and responded to. Those who speak out, no matter how irrational their words, may be revealing the truth of a situation. When spiritual leaders summarily dismiss criticism, either rationally or irrationally expressed, then arrogance dominates the exploration.

Emotion and outrage may obscure the truth of a perception, but that doesn't render it invalid. By staying silent in the group, by conforming to the silent majority, I passively grant leaders power and control over my life. I realize this is the very antithesis of spiritual freedom and the love and respect for integrity that flower from it. It is liberating to look at leaders as human beings, and not grant them supernatural status. Cult leaders' descriptions of themselves tend to seduce impressionable minds, but any serious inquiry into the structure of "self" doesn't leave much room for elevation of personae. It might be appropriate to steer well clear of groups for whom saying "yes" unreservedly is all that matters, though some people involved in cults may discover far more about themselves and codependent truth than those who remain on the sidelines. Joining any group is certainly rife with dangers, but never to risk an active form of spiritual exploration is remaining with the known and familiar. Can the seeker trust himself or herself to listen deeply and free himself or herself from notions of "in" and "out" and the preponderance of emotions and views that saturate these concepts?

The determination to live with wisdom, to tackle the forces of greed, anger and fear, pays respect to the forces of existence. There are opportunities to receive teachings. Breaking out of conventional ways of learning may not be as difficult as imagined. Those who are prepared to explore existence will not be bereft of wisdom and understanding. Recognition of wisdom without making it a basis for ego to build upon contributes to mindfulness, trust and purposeful action.

Seekers do not have to concern themselves with a big flash of enlightenment, though this is not outside the sphere of possibility. It is not necessary to adopt one interpretation of "reality." You do not have to have a changing or unchanging belief about the way the world is, or about what Truth is. Wisdom exposes the Emptiness of relative and absolute views. It isn't easy. Until you awaken you will be tossed about by circumstance, by the kaleidoscope of inner and outer forces. The irony of existence is that no matter how far you explore, how deep you probe you can never posit a final statement on the way things are. To do so is to restrict the Vast to a framework of language. You finally realize that religious, philosophical and scientific concepts do not say anything about anything. Yet if you don't explore, don't go into things, you will waste your existence because you opted instead for the mediocrity of mind's conditioned thoughts.

To find an answer to understanding life is missing the point. To find no answer to understanding life is equally missing the point. To impress upon others the "don't know mind" as the answer is providing an enormous disservice to others and ourselves. The champions of the knowing mind and the champions of the don't know mind are uncannily united in their opposing views. Ultimately, the packaging of words blinds you to your own experience of what is vast, inexpressible and uncreated.

Sky above,
earth below.
a breath
suffused the
whole galaxy.

CHAPTER NINE

GLORY OF A GODLESS SPIRITUALITY

GOD, that towering inferno of light, stands omnipotent. Elevated beyond mundane existence, God imposes His presence on the day to day struggle of believers. Words fail to describe His grandeur—a moral force, a holy presence, the supreme goodness, a transcendent realm yet expressing imminence. Supreme, Eternal, Transcendent, the Law Maker, the Creator of Heaven and Earth, Love and Truth—all belong to the impressive chain of concepts used to describe the Omnipotent One.

This complex existence with its good and evil wrought of human design is perplexing. In the matted framework of ideas and insights no social or political system approaches an adequate explanation, and beliefs and philosophies abound. Those of religious persuasion strive towards an experience of God. Sufferers and seekers, conquerors and vanquished, unable to make sense of their existence, or existence itself, discover a solution in God. One day comes a breakthrough, blowing away the previous speculations about existence: in God we trust. The Almighty becomes the supreme solution to everything. Like a bolt of lightning or, gradually, like climbing a mountain, we discover Him. He becomes a source of comfort, a faithful refuge, a resting place for volition and thoughts. When there are Divine revelations, believers overcome their anguish. The Ruler of Heaven and Earth grants His peace.

The words of saints, seers and enlightened ones speak with authority of His presence. The Holy Book, once regarded as a religious anachronism, becomes relevant describing the serenity of surrender. God uplifts the soul through His word. Like someone released from prison, we feel freed from a state of resignation to finite existence. God has come into our life and saved us from the pains of sin and karma.

The Light of the world comes at night, in dreams and in daytime. He comes in unexpected moments of prayer, in silence, in a crisis. The heart of the seeker becomes the heart of the lover, a joyful servant to the God that rules supreme. No words can convey the Sublime; so when God's presence enters our conventional ways of being He upsets the familiar balance of our lives. Things are never the same again. God has spoken not in words but through selecting various individuals of various faiths. We place ourselves in the hands of God.

We want to celebrate God by making His invisible presence visible. Cathedrals, statues, rituals, sacred books and religious paraphernalia become daily reminders of the call to God. How could anything possibly compare with finding the Supreme Being, knowing Him, surrendering and serving Him in this world and being with Him forever in the next world? It is all too easy to get lost in the world's problems with the endless travail through centuries of human and natural suffering. The Earth is a temporary domain, a short-lived preparation for the Eternal.

We want God to touch us so we can act in His name. Yet this seemingly irrational desire is beyond intellect and conventional thinking. We discard much to enter His house. We declare with conviction we have found God, that we were once lost but have become eternally grateful for God's presence in our lives. God is the commander-in-chief of circumstances, with lieutenants on Earth through whom He communicates. The circumstances of daily life belong to God's plan: He is the Loving Creator whose presence is all pervasive.

THEN COMES DOUBT. Despite all these experiences of God, we become racked with conflict. We start to doubt the existence of this Loving God whose divine plan permits such unbelievable terror and cruelty. We doubt this loving God who imposes such intense suffering upon the innocent and the guilty alike. This idea of a loving God gives rise to a great contradiction; such hypocrisy erodes the idea of God as an eternally benign and all powerful presence.

God is powerless to stop the human and environmental forces

that violate and desecrate the Earth. God is not All-Good, nor omnipotent. God is unable to prevent moral, physical and environmental pain. Unlike this Supreme Being, who remains aloof and untroubled by the nightmares of earthly existence, we feel deeply concerned about the brutality in life. We experience an inability to bridge the gap between the love of the Creator for his creation and the profanity of horrific suffering. We experience the disintegration of our belief in God. Perhaps God is not dead. He never existed.

Our original proclamations, the beliefs of others and sacred texts now appear deluded. How can we understand the contradiction of a Loving Creator and a brutalized world? God's lieutenants persuade people to interpret their inner spiritual feelings in a particular way and this stamps into the brain the language of God. Thus what we now disregard is a mind-made God.

The believers and the disbelievers condemn each other. The dualism of belief and disbelief haunts the mind looking into the apparent fragmented world. Children and adults die agonizingly from the cancers of industrialism and from famine and exploitation. The wars of bombs and bullets, the devastation from floods, the destruction of cities in earthquakes, and the ravishing of the Earth harm all life. We find that it is our spiritual duty to surrender our God in the face of these facts about life.

Who is willing to unload the whole religious package of seeking, surrendering and praising as nothing more than an attempt to fulfil emotional needs? Who is willing to listen to the voice of doubt? Doubt works its way through our investments in and addictions to the entire metaphysical structure of God. Yet notions of an All-powerful, All-merciful One are attempts to make sense of this life rather than deceive ourselves. Like science and philosophy, religion is an interpretation of Truth and we become embroiled in it to satisfy inner needs. Those diverse millions who have "found" God have a religious belief to guide their lives. Selfless love and compassion may flower from this experience regardless of whether God exists or is a myth. The existence or not of God is incidental to a deep, spiritual life. The inner worlds of perceptions with the concept "God" stuck in the middle can become states of religious hypnosis. Devotion, loyalty and faith can show as infatuation and existential comfort.

"Religious experiences cannot be explained." "We have to rely on faith." "God works in mysterious ways." We are told that unless we are willing to surrender, to give up all ideas of the way the Omniscient One works, we shall continue to dwell in darkness. When we find God we will act out His will. Out of this delusion we imagine we become holy and righteous and are prone to waging a war of words and actions on others. With the in-breath we claim God's will is unfathomable and with the out-breath we claim we know what He wants from us.

Out of our darkness we transfer our projections onto the image of a perfect, omnipresent God. Since we cannot be perfect ourselves we make up a God who is. Since we cannot know everything, we make up an omniscient God. We conspire to create a God, who is made in our self image and not the other way around. In this conceit we imagine we act from God. "It is not I but the Lord working through me". No amount of religious form, tradition, ritual, meditation or self analysis will liberate us from these mind games until we realize the emptiness of the God we have created.

Having the spiritual courage to renounce God, we have nowhere to turn and nothing to proclaim. Talk of purity through the experience of God sounds empty. A sinless life expresses an ideal removed from the rest of humanity. Abandoning all hope of being perfect, we submit to our conditioning, or explore our liberation free from the confinements of religious and secular beliefs. On the one hand we cannot cast aside the spectrum of invaluable experiences that occur in God's name. On the other hand, we unnecessarily fix this God to interpretations of spiritual experiences. Difficult emotions such as fear and aggression have diminished; love and compassion fill the heart. Dare we liberate ourselves from all our concepts of God as well?

Belief in the myth of God or God-as-Self requires an intense commitment. We bind our life around these particular notions. The issue is not the word "God" but the conception of God as a self existent entity. In the name of God, believers destroy entire cultures and environments. This particular image of God destroys the spiritual life as much as religious cynicism.

Where does it leave us? Our collective myths and legends, stories of miracles and spiritual powers, are implausible empirically and intellectually. The true miracle of life is walking on the Earth not on water. Yet we can respond to the Cinderella-type transformations announced by converts. We need not be cynical about myths and parables, and can understand their impact on human consciousness. The religious mind and the scientific mind are neither near nor far from the Truth.

One extreme position is claiming the Truth; the other extreme position is refuting the Truth or we take the standpoint that we don't know. Distinguishing fiction from fact, falsehood from Truth and the known from the unknown may jolt us out of the fairy tales we concoct about ourselves, others and God. That jolt might be remarkably liberating and joyful. We have the capacity to live without the name of God, without the name of His lieutenants and without reliance on self. Spiritual awakening refutes conventional wisdom.

Just as we have created a separate self existence we have created a separate God. We find ourselves acting in our name to get what we want or we act in the name of God. We have detached both our self and God from the moment to moment interconnection with phenomena. Time spent worshipping this divine God made in our image undermines spiritual awakening. Graven images of a Supreme Deity distort the world with its beauty and suffering. We exhaust the desire to perpetuate notions of the Deity; self interest often dominates such beliefs. We want to spare ourselves from the curse of theism, atheism, agnosticism and pantheism so we can explore deeply the spiritual life. We wish to be reverential to life and free from the sting of death. So the mystical tradition with its unprejudiced expression of enlightened wonder, joyful mysteries and indestructible friendship is revealed in our daily life. We also pay respect to the heart of the religious tradition, which spans thousands of years and is a source of inspiration for generations of spiritual seekers.

When we have abandoned the conception of God Up There we simultaneously liberate ourselves from the addiction of blindly believing in the literal truth of religious texts. Spiritual awakening discovers a peace that goes beyond conventional understanding and the fictional interpretations of our ego. The Emptiness of our constructed beliefs humbles us. We can never act in the name of Emptiness, nor serve, nor proselytize, nor become missionaries for it. In the face of mystical Emptiness God is dead, dogma is a distraction from the depth of mystery and love, consumerism is naiveté, national boundaries are lines in the mind. The ambitions and claims of self are pointless.

Emptiness does not offer anything new,
nor give licence to continue the old.
Emptiness reveals the lack of inherent existence of anything,
including itself.

Our brain is out of its depth. It is unable to comprehend the incomprehensible. We have nothing to say, no reference points and no pegs to hang our beliefs on. We have no central cause to champion. Our religion is silence and we have faith in our refusal to convert others. Ultimately all forms of religious and secular flag waving are empty activities of the mind. The search is over since the search itself had no true reality. The wonder of discovery and the wonder of nondiscovery are equally revealed. This depth of peace is like the peace of mind of the parent whose child emerges unharmed and happy from a coma.

Revelations and insights dissolve ignorance with its accompanying projections. The dream is over, and our deepest spiritual feelings towards what is awesome are revealed. The construction of the three letters G O D and the concoctions of associated beliefs evaporate. We cannot wrap our minds, nor our lives around this concept, for to do so would be sacrilegious, a profane act that neglects what is truly Profound. There is a blessedness; a benediction that our mind can never fathom.

CHAPTER TEN

RELIGION OF THE FLESH AND SPIRIT

In its anguish about the body, orthodox religion has never managed to enjoy the innocence and delight of physical beauty, sensuality and the highlighting of human features through cosmetics. Conservatives in the religious life view suspiciously ear rings for men, massage, nose rings, nude beaches, perfumes and saunas. As a result, religion has tended to promote an other worldliness with a suitably clothed Adam and Eve. This repressed reaction by religious authorities to physical attraction has contributed to religion's obsession with celibacy and condemnation of enjoying beautifying the body. One religious order refused permission for monastics to look at the body while taking a bath. Members of another order had to confess to other monks if they masturbated while others considered themselves sinful for experiencing the normality of sexual arousal. Organic molecular life became "the flesh", to be subdued and conquered.

Consumer society has elevated the body to a metaphysical status. Worship of the body has become a daily ritual, an act of devotion. Every region of the body—hair, eyes, nose, breast, chest, waist, genitals, backside, legs, feet—merits attention. The human organism has become an instrument for profit from head to toes. Endless "body" products persuade consumers to buy, buy and buy again. The desire to exist as long as possible and to impress others endorses worshipful attention to the body. Heaven can wait.

Products to pamper the body increase every year. The advertisers target every discomfort we share about features of our physical life. Manufacturers exploit and pamper every need. The list is endless—shampoo, conditioners, mousse, moisturizing lotion, nail varnish, nail varnish remover, liquid soap, mascara, lipstick, perfume, plaque remover, antiperspirant roll-on, shaving cream, night cream, hair spray, hair remover, wigs, sun tan lotion, sun blocks, sun beds, eye drops, ear drops, weight remover, face powder, hand lotion, body lotion. These products are manufactured to adorn and beautify—but market forces decide what is of value.

"Mirror, mirror on the wall who is the fairest of them all?" Morning, noon and night, the mirror becomes the reflection of fluctuating mental states about the body. Cosmetics promise to make us appear young and attractive. It becomes an increasingly uphill struggle to maintain the same appearance. Yet there is no indication that we are ány better off than those who have no access or use for such products. We often marvel at the bright, clear complexion of elderly nuns who have never used cosmetics. Perhaps creams clog the pores of the skin while chemicals enter the blood stream.

These materials, instead of being used with mindfulness and discernment, often become instruments to deny a changing process. A tiny but growing number of people even employ surgeons to restructure their physical parts. The wish to appear pleasing to others and comfortable with our appearance is natural, but today's society obsesses about the way nature has formed us. We deny the becoming process: youth leads to old age, to the withering and shrinking of the body; sensual beauty withers away leaving wrinkles, a spreading figure and greying hair. Health, vitality and vibrant sexuality change into a diminished energy and less interest in sexual intimacy. The desire to preserve the youthful state becomes a hopeless endeavour, a source of amusement for teenagers. Behind the infatuation with appearances lies insecurity. Frequently glancing in the mirror may or may not reassure us that we appear acceptable to ourselves and others. The consumption of vitamin pills, hunting for the right piece of clothing and endlessly browsing through fashion magazines reveal how far we go to feel good about ourselves.

Religion has been unwilling to marry the sensual forces of the flesh. Persistently the religious mind rejected the body, separating the spiritual from the physical, the soul from the sensual. Rejection of the body became a common article of faith among the world's religions. Integrated spiritual insights failed to register on those determined to deny the flesh its sensuous nature. Religions, East and West, still conspire to maintain this painful dualism of spirit and flesh. The world of the flesh belongs to the devil, to the unsatisfactory, while the world of the spiritual belongs to The Beyond, to God, to Truth.

Preachers and theologians still detail the sins of the flesh. "Men are sinners" is the rhetoric of the repressed, who say nothing good about natural physical feelings. Orthodox believers condemn the present age and regard it as permissive and irresponsible. The propagation of opinions continues at the expense of love, compassion and wisdom—the very ground of a meaningful religious life. This leads to opposing extremes—the desire to lengthen the time of our existence through fussing over the body and treating the body as sinful flesh. These two extremes lead to conflict and antagonism. Those obsessed with preserving their looks and sexual attraction cannot see further than their genitals while the others cannot see the relationship between their genitals and spiritual intimacy. The former only look downward and the latter only look upwards and both miss an opportunity for the marriage of flesh and spirit.

Missing the opportunity for harmonizing the spiritual with the sensual means living half a life. At times, we experience a thrust for life, an urge for intimacy and the awakening of the body—a genuine wonder and mystery of enlivening sensation. Our sexual energy is not subdued. Vows of celibacy do not repress it nor is it shackled through believing in holy vows of matrimony. The Sacred has nothing to do with marriage vows or celibacy but connects to ultimate realization. Vows are not carved into the nature of things; they are social or religious agreements. For some they are a constant challenge to the spiritual life because sexual feelings assert themselves in even the most sincerely religious mind. In the integration of mind and body, flesh and spirit, sexual feelings can express a sign of spiritual health not failure.

We may deny finding faith in the flesh and blood of intimate experience. If we do, then the spiritual will always struggle with the physical, one attempting to claim sovereignty over the other. No peace of mind and no joy emerge in such a struggle. Life becomes an effort to conquer passion in the name of the Sacred. The primordial nightmare of the religious mind is lust, and religious texts abound with heroic stories of the conquest of lust, the destruction of passionate urges and the denial of desire. It takes clarity and wisdom to understand the value of love and passion; unresolved problems around sexual desire require openness and insight.

Normal sexual responses challenge people in the spiritual life. These responses can be viewed as wretched corrupting failings, or as belonging to the wonder of human experience. An unsullied purity and celibacy do not necessarily have a relationship; purity is expressed in respect for ethical values, sustained kindness and an undemanding awareness. Retreat centres, spiritual communities and monastic institutions, adopt celibacy. Rightly understood, their purpose is not to suppress sexual feelings, but to give individuals the opportunity to experience aloneness and other expressions of deep intimacy. Sexual feelings rarely fade away for good. One value of celibacy is in allowing people the opportunity to explore the arising of sexual fantasies and the influence memory and projection play in relationship to the sexual experience. Celibacy has no special spiritual significance, but can help us face our aloneness in this world of birth and death.

Fading interest in sexual activity, usually a temporary phenomenon, is not necessarily bound up with spiritual development. Often the spiritual seeker has chosen other priorities that do not include a partner. So, at times, the variety of spiritual experiences, depths of meditation and intimacy with the environment may well include celibate existence. Others lead a celibate life because nobody is present and willing to start a sexual relationship with them.

Another difficulty around sex is the unwillingness to talk openly about it. It is still far more common for sex to be the subject of jokes and innuendoes. We have made a taboo of sex. The act is conducted behind closed doors while sexuality is often a closed topic. Repressed sexuality and promiscuity invite aggression, fear or guilt. Not surprisingly, sexual problems occur. Sometimes neither celibates nor sexually active people have insight into, or understand, their sexual experiences so the difficulties become accentuated. Understanding sex includes self knowledge, particularly of intentions, practices and attitudes, and the impact these have upon partners and social values.

When we invest in the "purity" of a guru, we risk disappointment later through revelations of his or her abusive sexual behaviour. It appears safer to invest our religious idealism in a person who has left this world; one who is physically dead. The living have a nasty habit of letting us down through living out their passions in harmful ways. The craving for attention and love can reveal itself in the desire for physical intimacy. The need for acceptance may result in submitting to somebody else's manipulation or aggression. Old feelings of isolation, failure or rejection make a person vulnerable to the dominating influence of another. Driven by emotions and needs, two people can have sex to give each other relief from the pressure, but it is a temporary relief and is no compensation for feeling relaxed with our sexuality. When there is undue pressure, no-one is secure. Sexual pressure leads to confusion and conflict through not realizing the impact of sex on another. Insight into the conditions that arouse sexual desire offers us protection and comfort. Sexual wisdom frees us from betraying, hurting and abusing others. Quick fix sex can make an unholy mess of the spiritual life.

It is appropriate to find caring ways of integrating the spiritual and physical passions. If we ignore this responsibility we are passively supporting the old struggle to make a seemingly ungovernable body governable. This reaffirms our judgements and hostility towards those bent on some private journey to physical intimacy. If we assume physical love is in a separate domain from divine love then the possibility for transforming conditioned perceptions remains out of reach. The willingness to affirm the religion of flesh and blood is the path to an integrated life.

So instead of faith being the unfounded hope for great things to come, an active faith involves participation in the Here and Now. What is happening in the living present is not dependent upon the words and behaviour of a religious authority, alive or dead. Perhaps it takes a substantial faith to explore the interconnection of experiences, to acknowledge the diversity of bodily sensations, to feel the sweetness of sensual pleasure, without fear, guilt or abuse. The Sacred manifests in the consequential and the inconsequential, and spiritual awakening pervades every cell, every nuance of this sublime existence.

We have to learn to be at home with our genitals and the life force that expands them, to regard those experiences as beautiful. We can bring into our awareness the countless factors that contribute to the arousal of the passions. We can reflect on the forms of denial and resistance from the past that still break out in the present. And we can remind ourselves that nature makes apologies to no-one for the strength of the life force manifesting through a human being.

Whatever emerges from our lives has its roots in nature. We are grateful for our sexuality, for the energies that it releases to a receptive heart and mind. There is room in the spiritual life, for sexual energies, whether we are sexually active or not. These energies do not block purity or threaten salvation. The experience of sexuality, alone or with another, is the very stuff of life, a religious happening in the interfusion of love and play. Life is celebrating itself.

The question arises whether the elimination of the old fragmented view of mind and body implies a swing to promiscuity. Spirituality revolves around our feelings and attitudes. Are the activities of the flesh contributing directly to the harming and exploitation of others? This form of sincere questioning contributes to sexually integrated lives. It is not easy to celebrate sexuality as an expression of something mystical and sacred. Faith, love and sexual expression can unite to reveal what is divine. The bedroom becomes a temple of joy, and Sacred Truth can be found equally between the bed sheets as in a holy book. Spiritual mystery and revelation are to be discovered in daily life experiences—in making love, cooking a meal, watering the plants, the quietness of the armchair. We venerate life as a state of deep spiritual intimacy.

The marriage of Heaven and Earth does not ignore any experience, and works towards assimilating the partnership of the spiritual and the physical into daily experience. Without this inner fundamental shift we live in isolation, forever championing the ideals of Heaven against the hold of the world, with a yawning chasm between. In ancient India religious artists strove to dissolve the gap between the worldly and the sacred by placing erotic sculpture in their temples. In Khadjuraho, tourists today stare at the figures locked in various poses of the sexual act. Few seem to register the significance of the interfacing of the flesh with the spirit. Some view the work from an artistic standpoint, others treat the work as purely erotic. Both miss the point. Eroticism, aesthetics and religious experience are not necessarily isolated, and together they can participate in profound awakening.

Sexual intimacy within a respectful communion touches a creative depth and a shared exploration between two people. The act may reveal the mysterium tremendum rather than just revelling in pleasurable sensations. Such shared moments are joyous expression of the wonder of life. To dismiss or judge the embrace of loving passion as desire or a procreative function says nothing about the experience, though it does say something about the perceiver.

Only the naive would give licence to any form of sexual experience to satisfy desire—even when reciprocated by another. Sexual experience is a heartfelt communication, worthy of utmost care and attention. By being fully respectful to each other, we have the opportunity to celebrate life through the sexual act. Such privilege ought not be treated superficially or with the cavalier attitude of the one-night stand. It requires an honest examination of our motives and an ability to perceive the feelings of another as well as our own. With reverence for the joy of another as much as for oneself, sexual love becomes a form of religious ecstasy. Reverence for life communicates itself through the rhythm and flow of physical intimacies which makes lovemaking spiritual, a meeting of the flesh and spirit. Each gesture, each move into further intimacy releases fresh energies into the moment. Two have become one, united in joy. Through reverence for life the body is free from mechanical activity. The pursuit of selfish sensual pleasure belongs to the divided world. Receptivity to sexual love brings Earth up to Heaven.

Prevented from transmuting the ordinary into the sublime the pursuit of the flesh is the pursuit of raw sensation. Two people become a tool for each other, a narrow fulfilment through embracing a sensation. The mind shapes the sensation and defines its perception through memory and image and the outcome is determination to fulfil desire.

To touch deep down in those moments of exquisite delight and love when body arouses body is to receive manna from Heaven; the inexplicable makes itself known in the flesh through a divinely physical communication. No wonder women and men yearn for such intimacies that embrace active reverence for each other. In these times of heart and body meeting, it seems as though all conceptual formations are irrelevant. Though the sensation of ecstasy fades into obscurity, a respectful awareness remains. The repressive worlds of religion and authority no longer matter. There is faith and wisdom in the religion of the flesh and spirit.

Part Three
Relationship to Perception

CHAPTER ELEVEN

A FIGURE OF SPEECH

The Earth accommodates around six billion people who share a wide-spread interest in exploiting the Earth's limited resources.
The Earth consists of more than 170 countries obliged to live together amidst an arsenal of ideologies and weapons.
The Earth is a small place which is becoming more overcrowded.
The Earth is a large place with room for everybody if resources are shared.

The nation state and states of mind dominate our perceptions of global life. Countries view their neighbours with trust, indifference, suspicion or hatred. Political and religious ideologies intrude into national perceptions affecting the way we relate to other countries; our views often reveal the influence of memory rather than a balanced appraisal of current situations. We do not trust the politics and religious beliefs of another nation, thus others cannot grant trust to our own questionable beliefs.

Places exist near and far; no possibility exists to visit them all and as a result much of the world never falls into our sphere of experience. We attach to the concept of "nation" that we form all manner of conclusions about people elsewhere, which can even become a licence to kill. By direct experience of a particular country, or indirectly through the perceptions of others, we form our opinions. Both leave lingering impressions. Yet we imagine we reflect the facts of a situation rather than limited information mingled with our state of mind. Upon what criteria are we able to arrive at a viewpoint? Our state of mind and the attitudes and beliefs of politicians and media set the standard for Truth.

Viewing others as living a long way away polarizes us, which gives rise to indifferent or dangerous metaphors. "The white man's burden," "The Yellow Peril," "The Iron Curtain," "The Silent Majority," "The Red Menace," all used extensively in recent generations, have fallen into disuse in contemporary language, but the damage remains. Psychologically the world is shrinking in size. Information technology, instant news and air transport influence perception despite the notion of objective distances between places. Global problems, such as the hole in the ozone layer, the greenhouse effect, destruction of tropical rainforests and population issues shrink the size of the world further. Yet owing to believing in objective distances between people the sense of intimacy fades quickly. The more we appear removed from each other, the less likely others matter. People viewed as living a long way away may not matter at all; if they don't, then it is impossible to engage in supportive activity with them.

Support for other people comes when we experience a shared connection with them. If we sense how small the world is, instead of how big it is, we feel closer to each other. This change of perception is not without risks; though it may touch upon friendly responses of support and mutual harmony, it may equally trigger fears of overcrowding and hostility. Not deliberating on these issues, we continue to assume the way we perceive the Earth reveals the way it is. By not reflecting on the differences between our perceptions, we conflict with others about what is objective. We struggle with and seek to undermine each other by imposing our perceptions. Closeness and intimacy become threatening. Too many thoughts about how close others are to ourselves may spark xenophobia. Immigration laws exclude foreigners—the hostility tied to the "not in my backyard syndrome" becomes a festering pit of paranoia. "Keep them out!"

Objective claims to distance become dangerous when thought of as inherently true instead of relatively. "Far" or "Near" need to be observed in relationship to values and states of mind. The emotionless responses by politicians and journalists to international events give an image of objectivity, but the public is deceived through this suppression of feelings into supporting the belief in independent facts. All people are worthy of consideration and acts of generosity, whether thought of as far away or near.

Words have no durable or universal meaning. The heart

deserves a major place in analysis of a situation. Neither places nor language have any objective reality. Opposite views reinforce our or others' views. Everyone imagines he or she is dealing with the real world and is in touch with the Truth. Since the Earth is neither large nor small, since places and people are neither near nor far, the observer's perceptions matter enormously. The notion of distances contributes to our thoughts, speech and action. Since the "world" is not one thing nor another, it is what we make of it. We do not need to make claims to objective truth. We need compassionate responses so there is instant marriage of heart and head in analysing any situation.

We claim we are living in the First World. We establish a distance between the First World and the Third World. We then believe Western society belongs to the civilized world. Our society sets the pace and we expect others to follow the road that leads to the First World. Repetitive use of language indoctrinates society into this way of thinking. We educate others to take the same steps we have taken so that they might arrive where we are. Abiding in our arrogance we subordinate others to our views, and by devaluing their lifestyles we set them on the road to our pathological prosperity.

I can only imagine that the daily interests of those on the other side of the world are not dissimilar from my own. I don't want to be subjected to a military invasion. I assume they don't. I don't want to have my home bulldozed over. I assume they don't. I don't want to go more than a few hours without a meal in my stomach. I assume they don't. I don't want to live in fear of the future. I assume they don't. I want my children to be able to get to hospital when they are sick. I assume they do. I want to feel free to express my concerns. I assume they do. I assume we all want to live in peace.

When I reflect on my relationship to others I doubt whether the idea "others" has any meaning. I see that common interests unite "I" and "others." Instead of buying into the usual metaphors that enforce blind stereotypes, we can use imagination to dwell deeply on the nature of human relationships. I wonder whether my fundamental daily concerns might apply to others as well? I cannot say for certain. I cannot make these inferences into convictions that form an ideology. What I make of the world and what I think are the same. People and places, items and issues at home and abroad, matter the moment I begin to think and speak about them. People and places cannot be separate from my views of them.

Ordinary everyday experiences, usually taken for granted, might be more insightful than we realize. Instead of a time-wasting search for some special experience to fill the demands of a dissatisfied self, we may instead take stock of the range of experiences forthcoming morning, noon and night. In any given moment countless others are sharing the same experience as myself. What can I discover from this experience? What do I need to understand from this? Awareness of the interrelationship of "I" and "others" alters our thought patterns and touches our heart. From this deep "place" I realize that others matter as much as myself. With this understanding experiences become the raw material for interpretations that could make a difference to the health and welfare of all beings on Earth, which is our home. It is the heart which brings us closer together in a meaningful way.

This fresh way of considering the Earth lends itself to wise action born of understanding the Totality of collective human experience. Where we perceive tyranny, cruelty, injustice and violence, we can respond, not with like-mindedness nor with passive acceptance nor "objective" facts but with active concern for justice, nonviolence, and appropriate change. We can explore boycotts and sanctions and other ways to halt those who deliberately bring suffering upon others. Nonviolence becomes powerful through collective protest, withdrawal of economic support and international cooperation. Ordinary experiences can be transformed into the liberating understanding of human experiences. Rather than participating in violent struggle, we can look into the nature of an experience and respond to Totality.

Using distance metaphors in the material world thus invites using the same metaphors for the spiritual world. The metaphors of "the path" and "the goal" occur with an obsessive frequency in the political and business worlds but also in the spiritual worlds. We then concoct the conclusion that "The Way" really exists as some independent entity that we can travel along. When language overshadows the Truth we become doomed to thinking in metaphors and acting upon those we identify with. Spiritual "paths" become significant in the perceived reality of distance. So we then indulge in such metaphors as "following the middle way", "I am the Way," or the "road to Truth". The seeker believes he or she is heading in the "right direction." Spellbound by time and distance metaphors of spiritual life we wonder how far along the spiritual path we are. With what instrument are we going to measure how far we have come? Whose perceptions are we going to believe? Are our conclusions based upon an unreliable feeling at the time?

Not only are metaphors an unsatisfactory basis for our spiritual life but they can also be painfully misleading. We may think we have fallen off the path, gone astray or been set off in the wrong direction. With our usual lack of investigation, we opt for the metaphor of path and goal as spiritual Truth. If upon examination a metaphor is empty of meaning then it can serve no purpose trying to measure where we are at, except to feel good or bad about ourselves. Not only do we form conclusions about ourselves on the path but also about others. We claim there are those who are on the right path and those who aren't, and those who have reached the goal and those who have not.

The use of "near" and "far," globally or spiritually, says as much about ourselves as it says about the place or path. We imagine a spiritual group or organization as a solid entity. We talk of "them", identify "them", group "them" and qualify "them." We imprison ourselves in words, believing words to be ultimate statements of reality, and are unable or unwilling to see the Emptiness of metaphorical language. And our tribal leaders and witch doctors—in the form of church leaders, royalty, doctors, judges, politicians and scientists—wage a war of words against those with different metaphors.

Intellectual games blind us to the influence of feelings which seem to substantiate our views. Pleasant feelings often may give rise to the idea of progress, unpleasant feelings to the idea of regression and in-between feelings to the idea of stagnation. With awareness of our feelings, thoughts and perceptions, there is less belief in the reality of where we are on the spiritual path. We start to see the notion of the spiritual path is not separate from the notion of a relationship to it, and both are often unexamined mental constructions. Then the investment in such mental constructions begins to lose the meaning and significance originally built up through idealizing metaphors.

We realize that there is no place to come from, no place to go to, and no place to stand on. The entire struggle to get something from clinging to a "spiritual path" loses its grip. The same wisdom also can be applied to a concept of "career," with belief in the metaphor of "working our way up the ladder." There is no path and no goal. Nobody has reached the top of the ladder. We abandon the mental constructions of path and goal, near and far, because we have realized that there is no inherent truth to these statements.

We may experience joy and contentment through witnessing the destruction of restrictive notions about ourselves. There is a taste of something different, something vast, not tied to the characteristics and methodology associated with following "the way." We awake to what is not time and place bound, and sense Immensity. But this is not guaranteed. We may experience unsettled feelings. The enthusiasm for being on the path and getting closer to God or Truth has dissolved leaving a spiritual aimlessness and uncertainty. If we grasp onto and identify with those unpleasant feelings, we invite divine discontent.

Through liberating wisdom, we experience a state of trust after abandoning teachings of the spiritual path and teachings of no-path. Then the opportunity for infinite discovery day-in and day-out is available. Nothing knows any real distance from anything else. Nothing is the same nor different from any thing else. The endless network of circumstances is the revelation of non-duality. Ultimate Truth appears obscured when the mind moves to give substance to time and place, path and goal. A heartfelt compassion emerges in realization of non-duality. There is an Intimacy with the vast network of circumstances that defies expression. Birth, death and the range of spiritual and worldly experiences do not affect this Intimacy.

CHAPTER TWELVE

THE LANGUAGE OF SELF-IMPORTANCE

The things we talk about are endless. Each time we speak we make something of this outpouring of words. Our conversations focus on about 40 topics, but our attitudes towards these topics may have frozen in time. We then continue to spout the same rhetoric year after year.

Our everyday talking points include: alcohol, animals, books, cars, celebrities, children, cities, clothes, cost of living, crime, desires, dreams, drugs, the environment, fantasies, fashion, food, friends, the future, the garden, health, holidays, jobs, life, love, men, money, movies, music, nations, neighbours, perfume, the past, politics, the powerful, race, relatives, religion, the rich, the royal family, sex, shopping, sports, television, towns, villages, war, the weather, women and work.

After speaking about these topics, we may wonder if there is anything else left. The ability to explore the serious issues of life, to converse about anything apart from habitual trivia, happens only rarely when certain circumstances have touched us. The rest of the time we love to recycle gossip. Our conversation is reduced to tittle-tattle about people and places without realizing we are perpetuating unsatisfactory communication—it is distressful for some people to be the subject of gossip. This feverish longing for gossip and spreading rumours generates what is referred to in Buddhism as *dukkha*—generally translated as "unsatisfactoriness" or "suffering"; i.e. "ill put-together."

Constant talking about situations makes them appear substantial. This reinforces the notion of an independent world referred to by an independent world of language. We fail to notice that the so-called objective world arises upon contact with its designation and description, and ceases with the ending of this description. We imagine that the real world divides into language and phenomena.

We occupy ourselves with the language of self-importance by speaking as if we always know best. If we derive pleasure in talking about a subject we like to repeat it to get the same pleasurable sensation. It gives us the feeling of knowing. We feel important. We bring a range of perceptions to embroider the topic and gain a peculiar satisfaction in relaying to others our likes and dislikes through chatter.

Daily indulgence in small talk contributes to a flighty mind, uncontrolled tongue and frivolous attitudes. Through insights into our conceited conversations we gain wisdom; egotism does not then impregnate the matter under discussion. Then small talk finds its place. When a situation appears as difficult or heavy we have the opportunity to be mindful of the importance attached to the situation. By dwelling obsessively on a "particular" we perceive it as substantial, as mattering more than anyone else or anything else at that time. When a topic has become this important we have granted "it" independent existence. Importance has desire as its background, foundation and primary cause. We crucify ourselves in desire for a person, position or things seen as important. The resulting pain and anguish intensify substantiality and selfhood. Tears shed in humankind's history through unfulfilled obsessions would fill the world's oceans.

What use is language if it only reinforces problems and the notion of separate, independent existence? Language seems to give substance where substance does not exist. When "something" is seen inherently to exist it seems worthwhile pursuing or avoiding. Yet the existence of "something" is subject to change, to becoming other than what it was. All "things" only have an existence through the support of everything else. Communication can be employed to inflict pain or dissolve it. We can point out lack of self and let go, instead of clinging to a mythical self—be in silence instead of chattering. The purpose of communication is not to ramble on, or even philosophize about the nature of the world, but to end the compounding of suffering, and the language of self-importance.

A woman reflecting on such themes once approached me and said: "I like suffering. Suffering is important. Why should I want to get rid of suffering? Suffering is part of life. Everybody suffers. I don't mind suffering. Why should I want to exclude such a basic truth of life?" I said: "How are you feeling right now?" She replied: "Right now, I'm feeling fine. My life seems to be going along rather well." She continued to reassure me that she had no objection to the suffering in her life; regular suffering was in the "natural order of things." She said it was "unnatural not to suffer. Anybody who sees the end of suffering is closing themselves off to a wonderful part of life."

I told her she was speaking in the abstract and from an intellectually safe posture. I told her to come back and make the same remarks when she was experiencing suffering. Some months later she appeared at my door in deep distress. Her husband had walked out on their marriage and found a lover half his age. Rage, jealousy and despair consumed her. I reminded her of what she had told me some time previously. I added: "I assume this is a substantial issue for you. Are you interested to end suffering right now? Do you wish to cling to the viewpoint that says 'Suffering is a wonderful part of life. Why should I want to get rid of my suffering?' Isn't your deepest wish right now to be free from all of this suffering you are going through?" She agreed wholeheartedly.

Bewitched with words, spellbound by language, we support all manner of claims and beliefs about the way things are. We nail our reality to events only to be forced to change our views when circumstances change. We take pride in our views, thinking we are rather smart and others are rather dumb. We form certain beliefs about ourselves and observe others to see if they view us in the same way. What they say to our face or behind our back affects us because this deeply rooted idea of "I" arises and enters our perceptions. "I" think about myself and "I" think about what others think about "me." We believe in our own superiority—or lack of it.

Pride, this idea of a superior self, no matter however humbly expressed, claims "I am better than you." Alongside the conceits involving "I" is the desire to win the attention of others, to appear significant to those we wish to impress. Frequent expression of our conceit becomes a form of unconscious boasting and subsequent arrogance. Once this pattern is established, we become intolerant of criticism. A barely concealed hostility is directed towards those who do not believe in our "self" importance.

When the spiritual leader gave his lengthy talks he frequently felt compelled to mention that he was enlightened. Sitting in a huge chair and surrounded with flowers, he began to gain more self-importance. Believers looked to him to tell them how they should spend their lives. He told his followers that what he was doing was going to be very big (in a world of six thousand million people?). More and more of his sentences began with the word "I." He told his followers that nonbelievers were not ready for him. Nonbelievers felt the guru was not ready to teach.

A couple, with young children, said that they had found The Truth, they became enlightened through surrendering to him. They had realized that all the striving to find the Truth had been a complete waste of time. "To be free one had to surrender. It was the only way. Having unconditionally surrendered one abides in the Truth," they said. The couple were very sincere, very happy and it appeared that something particularly precious had happened to them. They expressed gratitude for the teachings they had received in the past, and particularly from their guru.

The wife said: "I am no longer afraid of death. Death has lost all meaning for me. Death is just a change of circumstances. That is how it is for you, for me, for everyone. There is nothing to fear when death has no meaning." She spoke in an assured way. I asked her if she had been close to death recently. Not since she had totally surrendered, she responded. I asked her about her children. She said she loved them very much. They meant a lot to her. I asked her if it would not be wise to be a little more provisional about her claim that death had lost all meaning for her. She replied with a little agitation that if I had the same realization I would say the same.

I replied that to identify with events such as death by investing them with meaning or by negating meaning was not my way of teaching. I asked her to reflect on her relationship as a mother to her child. Death is separation from what we hold most dear. The metal of bold statements is tested in the fire of circumstances.

I said to her: "If you died today you would leave behind your children. What would be the effect on them attending their mother's funeral? Your husband would have to cope with the sorrow and pain of both himself and his kids. Death is separation, probably forever, from all those that you love most dearly." Tears came to the eyes of the woman. "The significance of death hadn't occurred to me in that way. I was just thinking for myself," she said.

The nature of things has a remarkable capacity to force us to examine what we believe. Our beliefs are not separate from the vast process of existence. Scientists have claimed that if we were able to throw a ball hard enough in one direction of the universe it would eventually come round and hit us on the back of the head. We may not experience that with a ball but it certainly seems to occur when we throw out egotistical claims about ourselves.

Only the naive believe in self-exultation. Pride, arrogance and hypocrisy tend to arise from dearly held beliefs. Beliefs become cherished and nurtured as reality, owing in part to the desire to feel self-important. The desire to fulfil our wishes comes from viewing the world in terms of what is pleasant and unpleasant, satisfactory and unsatisfactory. Getting what we want from religious experience matters more than realizing the emptiness of egotism.

Once we have taken an absolute stand on our religious beliefs we blind ourselves to a larger vision. We can neither see nor hear others, nor understand them. In awakening we comprehend how we subvert experiences and insights to self interest. Failing to understand how all circumstances dependently arise, we tie ourselves to a conceited self, who has found the Truth. By not grasping onto spiritual experiences, we do not form rigid standpoints of existence. By not attaching ourselves to views, nor detaching from them, we realize that the end of perception and feelings is the way out of this bewitchment with the self.

Not regarding a particular standpoint as the best, not condemning the views of others, the wise go beyond the limitations of views. The dogmatist invests in views for a feeling of self worth, but through honest investigation we discover the relationship of self-importance to dogmatism. We can then respond to our deep experiences with wisdom instead of dogma. There are those who prefer to quote the authority of a book or person to support their own argument. This is one way that views beget views.

Preoccupation with praise and blame, superiority and inferiority, security and insecurity is a noticeable characteristic in the world of self-interest and egotistical language. Bound up in such a world, we continue to believe we are dealing with the Truth, and cannot see further than our thoughts. Spiritual awakening treats a thought as a thought.

When language and forms cease to designate the ultimate nature of things then consciousness associated with language and forms also ceases. When all language is abandoned then all phenomena is abandoned, then all ways of speaking are abandoned. Release from the grasping tendency to name and believe, to label and describe, to pinpoint and specify leaves nothing to be said. Perceptions and feelings, consciousness and content, words and beliefs, the pleasant and the unpleasant cease to have any ultimate significance. The "I" has nothing to build on. For those who have exhausted their appetite for involvement in the limitations of names and forms, words and impressions there is neither withdrawal from that world nor infatuation. "The world" has as much substance as language designates. Words are nothing in themselves but are only tools for the world of conventional appearances.

Ultimately, words tell us nothing about anything, not even about words, whether the language is everyday, metaphysical, psychological or scientific. Relative perceptions are tied to the everyday world. There is the opportunity for liberation from views and opinions. Consciousness tied to the everyday world of self, others and the world cannot comprehend the Ultimate Truth. When this preoccupied consciousness collapses we understand moral, emotional and spiritual awakening. The obsession with issues is punctured.

Realizing the Emptiness of viewpoints, conventional or metaphysical, is not the sole purpose behind spiritual awakening. Spiritual awakening reveals the foolishness of personal claims on Truth. Insights into Emptiness are liberating and it is this liberation which matters, not the Emptiness of the viewpoint. To offer a view of Emptiness might give some sense of purpose and meaning to life. But it does not lie at the heart of awakening. Spiritual enlightenment refutes a position of no view. No view states a view. Objects of perception, objects of meditation become unimportant since no word can say what an object truly is—or even if it is. The formations of nouns, verbs, adjectives and participles do not say anything about anything: even poetry cannot truly describe the nature of things.

We also abandon the view that Reality underlies words and things. What presents itself is language and phenomena. Both lack any self existence. Neither is more real than the other since both are mutually dependent. Lacking in self-existence, words have neither more nor less reality than what they dare to describe. Something and nothing are the playthings of the conventional mind. In the world of names and forms nobody is further from or closer to the Truth. Since nothing contains any inherent self existence there is no basis for descriptions or theories. There is "no-thing" to describe. We cannot speak of That which ultimately cannot be described.

As a functional activity, language shows its limitations as much as its relative use. A large vocabulary and extensive knowledge impress us. We wish we were as articulate as others. No matter how many new words we introduce into the language, they will not bring us one iota closer to the nature of things. We express countless views and opinions every time we open our mouths but profound realization awakens the organism to an extraordinary sense of the Ultimate Truth of things. The world of relevant words for relevant situations appears as irrelevant.

At times we feel misunderstood and experience the frustration of struggling to get across what we want to say. But if we *feel* our way into our central ideas we may see that the religious beliefs or experiences we are attached to invite the opposite response from others than we want. We cannot abandon these concepts owing to the need to build up our self-importance. We might stop feeling important and we don't want to experience that. We frequently deceive ourselves and others when we imagine we are keeping alive a sacred message in the world. Charged concepts give our life meaning. The investment and clinging to charged religious concepts does the opposite. Clinging to beliefs renders *life* meaningless.

In the conventional world, we designate experiences as belonging to self, the experiencer. "I had this experience." When this possessiveness around experiences happens—as it often does —we forget that sensations arise owing to contact and stop when contact stops. The appearance of "I" and "my" appears in the process of contact, feelings, and states of mind. When we distinguish "my" suffering from the suffering of others we inhibit the capacity to see through "I" and "my." With awareness and insight into the unfolding process we witness a change from "my pain" to "the pain" to "pain". The vision, expansive and profound, knows no isolation. "I" and "my" is without essence. We see that suffering arises neither from myself, nor another but from contact.

Mental constructions are nothing more than a string of thoughts, an attempt to describe appearances. Once having named something, "it" becomes something to continue, change or negate. The cessation of suffering is the ending of names and forms, the ending of consciousness and content. The end of suffering is immediate, not in the realm of metaphysics. The revelation of the ending of name and forms is not apart from names and forms. In the unborn mystical process Emptiness reveals moment to moment contact.

To take the above up as a theory renders every sentence a waste of time. To identify with any passage is to grant it self existence. To reject any passage gives self-importance to the reader's views. In realizing the Emptiness of any self existence and self-importance we respond with wisdom and kindness to what we see all around us.

CHAPTER THIRTEEN

PERISH THE THOUGHT

Thinking is often at the forefront of our inner life. Our thoughts intrude into areas where they have no business, indulge in matters outside their scope and seize onto conclusions no matter what the cost. We think obsessively about a wide range of ideas and champion self-opinionation. We mull over countless issues but remain blind and indifferent to the process of how we think. We use judgmental language that disempowers our listeners or readers and can hinder their thought processes.

Thought—the mental faculty of concepts, words, images and ideas—makes its presence felt in every sphere of conventional existence. Thoughts frame events and circumstances; thoughts also determine the significance of events. Yet we rarely watch the thought process itself. Despite our capacity to fabricate all sorts of conjectures about life, we avoid looking dispassionately at our thoughts. We become glued to our thoughts through the repetition of certain streams of thought. We fix our life into a particular interpretation. The ending of identification with the thinker expands life beyond this frame. When we dissolve this sticky identification our experience of life is expanded. The doors of perception are opened. The key is the choiceless observation of the streams of thoughts.

We can ask ourselves:

What process occurs that enables thoughts to become compounded into fixed ideas?

What is the result of clinging to our ideas?

What happens to consciousness when we witness fully the appearance and passing of successive thoughts?

When we are not looking at life through our thoughts what is the nature of our experience?

Our blindness relies upon our mind forming opinions and drawing conclusions. Thus we fail to comprehend the totality of each question, its ramifications and the widespread consequences of the answer. We have become a product of our thoughts, thoughts give shape to the kind of world we experience.

The university professor admitted to his spiritual teacher that he lived in the world of books. He had accumulated a small mountain of them. He thought about his subject, gave lectures in his chosen field and saw the world through his knowledge. As an authority in his field, he held a prestigious post in a top university. No matter how much the professor tried to examine his thoughts he found that he kept forming habitual views and opinions about himself and his relationship to his social world. He was a prisoner of his way of thinking. The spiritual teacher set him a task for a year. He told him to starve his thoughts through a single act of austerity by taking a year's sabbatical and abandoning reading for 365 days.

The professor agreed to the task which forced him to confront a lifelong habit upon which he based his education, career and self-evaluation. In the first weeks, he found himself unwittingly reading the small print on the packet of cornflakes at the breakfast table. He would find himself staring at other people's newspapers on buses, or reading graffiti in public toilets. Starved of words, his life felt purposeless at first, but as time went by he began to see that information did not reveal the nature of the world but hid it.

He began to see the relativity and limitation of his sphere of knowledge. The relationship of consciousness to the world revealed itself in fresh ways. Insights and realizations about thought, knowledge, its functions and limitations became apparent. The professor left the university, the corridors of knowledge. He had arrived at the end of knowledge. His vast repertoire of thoughts would never mislead him again,

Immediate access to the world is through contact with the five senses; sight, sound, smell, taste and touch. Almost simultaneously, the mental faculties perceive an object. In that moment, the world of self and other, consciousness and content, subject and object arises. The world appears through contact with consciousness. In the moment of perception the object or sensation influences consciousness. Perceptions form a dualistic world of human being and objects. Past impressions influence how we experience present sensory information. So consciousness, perceptions, feelings and past influences all manifest themselves. Our thoughts begin to solidify and we begin to think that we have to preserve the object of interest, change it, observe it, develop it or let go of it. Whenever a thought repeats we tend to think of it, or its object, as "something-of-itself." Once this has occurred the world of for and against, likes and dislikes, coming and going, is born.

Thoughts depend on the state of body, consciousness, feelings and perception. Throughout numerous moments of the day occurrences register in the mind. Only a handful of the daily stream of impressions are taken up, made something of and become objects for preoccupation. We can become obsessed with the content, feelings and emotions present. Preoccupation with our thoughts focusing around a belief, a goal or a fantasy can last indefinitely, while the original trigger for the thoughts may have been quite brief.

To watch thoughts rather than follow them, and to explore their influence provides insights into our world view. For example, supposedly well-made plans safeguard the mind against confusion, purposelessness and despair. We would rather not admit that our obsessional deliberations are born of insecurity. What we see, hear, smell, taste, touch, remember or dwell on needs thought for continuity. Yet there are ways we can think about our concerns that are precise, skilful and free from fear and desire.

Binding ourselves to thoughts leaves us estranged from deeper feelings about life. We do not observe the spark of our philosophies. Calculating thought becomes devoid of feeling. Cold, hard and analytically oriented towards efficiency, we carry a ruthless determination to achieve goals. Thought becomes an isolated, intransigent modus operandi with life viewed as subservient to the demands of our views. We become estranged from sensitive feelings and abide in a world of attachment to ideas and indifference to others.

The interests of self mould our thoughts so they become charged with prejudiced interest. Wisdom can be the equivalent of terrorizing such conditioned thoughts until we explode into a fresh awareness of the nature of things. The determination to explode hardened thought is vital in the heart's opening to an expansive vision of life. Habits begin like cobwebs and become cables.

It is not enough to forgive other people or ourselves for not knowing what we are doing. Blindness and ignorance cause suffering, so awareness and investigation into harmful behavioural patterns is a human duty. An attitude that seeks neither to exploit, harm nor violate the world characterizes such investigation. The quality of our action matters more than the results we pursue. Infatuation with the achievement of our aims can persist despite the fallout in personal or global life. Genuine awareness and insight into the total activity of body, speech and mind enhance life.

Wise thoughts are appropriate for an attunement to life that is in accord with the nature of things. Reverence for life, compassion and gratitude give support to healthy thoughts. In this process we experience our heart, mind and the world living in harmony. Wise thoughts contribute to the welfare of the world only at the expense of greed, aggression, fear and delusion. The clinging, grasping mind lacks trust and openness. At times the struggle is between various forces of self-interest. In the past people have been violated in ways that have left them clinging more strongly to self-interest. Attitudes towards others can have a long term impact.

Our continual self-interest feeds reaction, desire and aggression in others. We inflict our reactivity upon others, our loved ones, and ourselves. The ability to deal wisely with the interests of self comes through wisdom about life not through attachment to our position. Attachment can unleash fear and aggression inhibiting a considerate understanding.

We experience an initial impression and initial thought. This serves as a springboard for reaction. Owing to impulses, patterns, memories, and emotions, we begin to think and behave in a way which obscures and blinds us to understanding what is going on. Any form of clinging or attachment does not serve mutual well-being but only perpetuates the conflict of self and other. Our thoughts express our underlying behavioural patterns and psychological roots. The way we think is the way we act—our stream of thoughts is none other than internalized action. Mental entanglement accompanies the belief that endless thinking will uncover a solution. This obsession is pointless, yet the force of the momentum to keep on thinking continues. Thus the activities of negative behaviour continue. There are certain aspects about thought processes we can look at:

Be clear when we are identified with our thoughts.

Establish our capacity to be mindful human beings.

End indulgence in flights of fancy, day dreams and meandering thoughts.

Be aware of feelings, intentions and perceptions that support thoughts.

Be mindful of the thoughts about thoughts.

Be aware of negative thoughts and caring thoughts and know the difference between the two.

Remember that a thought is just a thought.

Monitor the thoughts, regard them as belonging to a process rather than the thinker.

The computer expert would never admit to himself he was a workaholic. He was in his late 20s, working 60 hours or more a week and earning a substantial salary. If the company expanded at the present rate, he would become a millionaire in five years. For that to happen he had to work hard and continue to buy shares in the company. The office was buzzing with activity as his ambitious colleagues strove to climb the conceived ladder of success.

He told me that he seemed to exist 60 hours a week from his head upwards. Worse, when he got home at night he habitually turned on the television. About one evening a week he went to the cinema. "I'm a prisoner of the screen" he told me. "I'm not living in the real world. I'm living in the world of letters, figures, graphs and images. I've noticed I hardly laugh at a comedy show any more or get upset at seeing gratuitous violence on the television. I'm hardly aware of my wife and young children. I've become an automaton, a pawn in the business world."

Serious dangers face us when we become restricted to the rigidity of thought formations, cerebral activity and a mechanistic lifestyle. There is loss of access to the deep, inner feelings and intimations of life. Through lack of expression the heart begins to shrink, feelings dry up. Order, timetables, efficiency, accuracy and goals replace spontaneity, humour, love and affection. We frequently cannot accept that this is the situation even when it is perfectly obvious to those around.

We become obsessed over details. A sense of perfect order is employed to maintain the status quo through a sustained denial of inner reality. Heartless and ambitious, we treat with disdain those who are kind and unselfish. Rational, controlled thoughts conflict with the feelings and emotions of another. Once thought has been in exile, the road back to an integrated and heartfelt life is a challenging adventure and a matter of urgency: the well of deep feelings for life can run dry. Life is not a rehearsal. We need to listen to the feedback we receive from others. Are we being told regularly that we are lost in our heads, cut off from our feelings, unable to show loving and compassionate emotions? Isolation from our feelings and concentration upon cerebral activity leads to articulate computerized human beings, who supply all the right answers. The cost is the loss of a joyful, spontaneous and celebratory existence.

A healthy psyche expresses honesty, generosity, kindness and compassion. To know ourselves and find out about ourselves involves taking risks, inviting feedback and responding to it. Yet we are fooling ourselves and others by believing we can pursue all our material aspirations without consciousness and organic life paying a devastating price.

We can experience the struggle of one set of thoughts over another, one part of ourselves differing from another. We wonder why on Earth we are doing what we are doing, yet other thoughts drive us on relentlessly. In such duality, our thoughts oppose each other, the mind is haunting self with its unresolved conflicts. We think the mind has separate parts with each one having an inherent or independent existence in contrast to the others. We continue in conflict because, tragically, we lack courage to change and prefer to live in desire and fear. The ability to stop the remorseless train of thinking is vital; thus we can experience a genuine connection with our world that is inseparably linked with our life. We have the opportunity ...

to breathe mindfully,
to abide with generosity,
to be available for friends and strangers,
to be gladdened with understanding that thoughts are not everything,

to celebrate,
to observe with interest and appreciation the perennial unfolding
characteristics of existence.
to see the flaws in our philosophies and failed master plans.
to realize an enlightened life.

The objectifiers of the world become correspondingly bound to ideas. First they dwell exclusively on an idea and then promote it. Of such stuff dreams are made. We can wake up to realizing that our entire package of thoughts is feeding the problem not curing it. Believing we are part of the cure, and not part of the problem, is potentially a dangerous thought—a short step away from intolerance and fanaticism.

The world becomes a backdrop to the endless bickering, squabbles and fighting over the supremacy of particular thoughts. Understanding the relativity of thinking leaves a vast space for exploring the mystery of life and compassionate action, inaccessible to hardened opinions and unavailable to a conditioned life. The professor put aside the world of information for such liberating discoveries; our challenge is to dismiss all distractions.

CHAPTER FOURTEEN

WISE FRIENDSHIP

To understand the relationship between ourselves and the world is to explore the interaction of sensory information and inner experience. Understanding this interaction contributes to peace and joy. Those with wisdom enjoy the tremendous trifles of daily life born of the interaction of events. This embrace of the mystical permeates feelings, thoughts, perceptions and actions. Such full-bodied experience penetrates the senses and gives a quiet background of support and calmness to the sensory sensations suffusing eyes, ears, nose, tongue, and body, known as the five sense doors.

Mindfulness leads to an interest in the world of sense impressions interconnected with inner experiences. The world of touch includes contact with the elements—the soil underfoot, the warmth of a child's hand, raindrops on the face. The willingness and interest to experience Intimacy reduce preoccupation with desire and possessiveness. By giving a choiceless attention to each sense door we reduce desire for the particular sensations connected with ownership and consumption.

Preoccupation with accumulating possessions is living in the dark ages, a closet-consciousness unable to see the harsh reality of the decline of natural resources. Shrugging off the dishonourable pursuits of consumer religion turns the world into hallowed ground for insight and revelation. The dynamic interplay of the five elements with consciousness becomes a magical mystery tour. Earth, air, heat, water and space are integral to the human being and the environment.

Loss of one of the senses heightens sensitivity of another. If someone loses his or her eyesight, the other senses develop in compensation, becoming acutely aware of the surrounding world. Mindfulness, interest and energy are naturally directed to the remaining four senses to handle the immediate world as skilfully as possible. Wisdom is concerned with the mind's interaction with sense objects for a full bodied friendship with all forms of life. We see life's idiosyncrasies, absurd contradictions and utter inability to meet our expectations. The actions of others that appear incongruous and irrational do not daunt or dismay friendship. Awareness of circumstances unleashes a vigour for life. Whether let down, judged and ignored, those who abide with an understanding of change are slow to be moved to anger. They remain undaunted because awareness pervades the mind's movement.

Friendship does not seek continuity, nor demand something in return, but is perpetuated through its own momentum. Those undaunted by circumstances and undismayed by events have a presence like a positive germ that is infectious—touching others in ways that are hard to comprehend. The combination of kindness and awareness can penetrate the innermost world of another and strip away their defences. Body language, gestures, eye contact and speech are physical expressions of this inner peace; warmth can melt the fears and defences of others.

Creatures are also receptive to affection. An expansive friendliness towards all living beings removes the wish to destroy other life forms; we feel enamoured of the animals, birds and fish which grace the Earth with their presence. We appreciate the sight and sound of their freedom, wishing them the right to live their life as undisturbed as possible by that thinking—or is it unthinking?—human creature. Emanating warmth and kindness, we embrace the natural world with its sun and rain, oceans and puddles, tropical rain forests and house plants, countryside and deserts. By not displaying hostility towards one climate and lauding the praises of another, we appreciate the diversity of the natural world. From this affection right action emanates, born of awareness and concern for the natural world, animals and humans.

When desires hound our life, we experience the diminishing of kindness and consideration, and the spectre of disappointment overshadows what is naturally good and beautiful. Within human relationships we can sometimes observe a significant inability to accept or recognize another. We also may treat others, animals and nature for our personal ends. But this negative behaviour only persists, if we sustain our belief in the mental construction of *us and them*.

Resentment, aggression, hatred and violence eat away insidiously at all levels of awareness and wisdom. We cling tenaciously to opinions about good and evil, right and wrong, which we take as self-evident. The selective information manipulates our views instead of contributing to a comprehensive awareness of situations. Biased information becomes more important than the Totality. We reinforce our views through the eyes of hostility. Blinkered reactions darken perceptions and condone the duality of us and them. Every aspect is involved in the production of friendship and violence.

Anger operates on the premise that we are (or I am) right and they are (or he or she is) wrong. Preserving this position at all costs generates dark moods of aggression. Not only does anger get aimed at those who are conceived to be cruel, blind or power hungry, but spreads inexorably to others as well. Like a sudden storm, anger can rain upon everyone without discrimination. The person angry about social injustice may even believe that his or her commitment to justice is stronger than that of those who prefer direct action through awareness and love.

When anger is felt to be justified it hardens views and opinions. Rage is not far away. "I feel angry and I have a right to be angry" is the slogan of the frustrated, the hurt and the disappointed. Perpetuating this attitude only adds to the anger already present in the world. Righteous anger nourishes the us and them duality until it is perceived as the only reality. We may fail to recognize the interdependence of circumstances. To be serious about reducing violence requires understanding the way anger and militant accusations contribute to it. Like a harmful germ, hostility has the capacity to spread at an alarming speed.

Belief in the right to act from self-righteous militancy highlights an emotional pattern that needs an object to latch upon. Anger over issues is understandable, and it is likely that a concerned person will feel angry in the presence of painful information. But when we justify and rationalize anger, we grant it momentum. We begin to see fault everywhere. We circulate among a clique who share our hardened views and perpetuate them, or we withdraw into a state of sullen moodiness. We exhaust our potential for deep friendship and the willingness to deal with matters in fresh ways. We lose our capacity to examine patterns of aggression in ourselves and others. Anger can then explode into rage or fury, violating life and wisdom, and even reinforcing the people and systems we hate. We also forget how to laugh, play and be happy.

We think we are right. Yet our inflamed mind and the intensity of our self righteousness is ironic: we think and act in the same way as those for whom we reserve our greatest wrath! Like breeds like. What *they* have done is what we are moving towards doing. Personal, social and global history repeats itself until consciousness is transformed. Until then the difference between us and them is only one of degree. By excluding ourselves from responsibility we launch our missiles of words or metal against others, exhibiting the same behaviour and using the same justifications as those we attack. We feel strongly that we have good reasons. So do they.

Everyday irritations provide the basis for insights into the latent tendency of viewing a world of goodies and baddies. Our cowboy mentality cannot comprehend that it is as much a part of the overall problem as believing it is part of the cure. When we are absolutely certain of holding the correct view we fail to see the consequences of such a position. By looking judgmentally at another person's behaviour, the mind loses the ability to act wisely and explore skilful ways to solve the issue. All that we perceive is the effect on ourselves or others and that is enough to wind us up.

Perhaps we think we know what they are doing and why they are doing it. It is as though we regard ourselves as mind-readers able to fathom the innermost workings and considerations of someone else's actions. We ignore the person's previous experiences, other events going on in their lives and what they bring to the situation. When pinpointing the faults of others, we expect a positive response instead of hearing reactivity. Fault-finding lacks consideration for the influential circumstances of another's situation. Both the accuser and the accused believe they are doing the right thing or at least what is necessary. Our rage and condemnation fail to acknowledge conditions, past and present, inner and outer that affect their behaviour.

Two hours before the flight departure passengers are queuing with their luggage to check in. As a passenger reaches the desk, having spent 15 minutes in the queue, the desk clerk apologizes. She says her booking desk is closing and tells people to join the queue at the next desk. The passenger blows up. "I've been standing here for ages. Why didn't you tell me before? Don't you realize that I have a plane to catch. If this is the way you treat passengers I'm going to take my custom elsewhere," he yells at her. The desk clerk says nothing, assembles her papers and leaves the desk. Who knows what is going on in the lives of the passenger and the desk clerk? Yet we tend to judge both.

The witness to the situation frequently takes the single event and isolates it from the totality of events, past, present and future. The point is not to justify the abuse of the passenger or the withdrawal of the desk clerk. It is to see whether the mind is immediately taking sides in a dispute, the grounds upon which it does and the attitude formed towards those involved. Neither a detached view nor a sympathetic view is particularly virtuous. Our attitude, emotional and intellectual responses both parties matters as well.

While witnessing such a dispute, we may desire to tell those involved what we are thinking, but often, rather than risk a nasty rejoinder, we keep quiet, stiff upper lip firmly in place. Distancing ourselves in a safety zone may postpone a one-sided reaction, but to take sides only adds wood to the fire. What we fear to say directly we say behind their backs. Backbiting is a favourite pastime of the fearful; it is less risky to mutter nasty comments out of the side of our mouth. Knowing when to speak up and when to remain silent requires a wisdom free from the duality of us and them. In a state of reaction the primary interest is to get others to agree with our perception of a situation.

The young world traveller had taken slide after slide of sights his eyes had feasted upon. His cameras, with wide angle and zoom lenses, plus hundreds of slides and numerous rolls of unprocessed film, accompanied him everywhere. On a train in Asia the bag and its contents disappeared along with eighteen months' worth of used film. "I never should have come here. They are nothing but a bunch of thieves. You can't trust any of them. You'll never catch me there again. If I were you I would be very careful if you meet anyone from this part of the world. They'd steal from their own mother." Unable to cope with loss, unable to see that there is no relationship between thieving and continent, the mind spins into a destructive orbit in which latent prejudices surface. A personal experience becomes the justification for abusive generalizations.

Friendship diminishes with frustration. We suffer endlessly through the inability to get what we want, to recover what we have lost. Seemingly betrayed by circumstances, we become enshrouded in negative perceptions. The erosion of thoughtful action has a history of unexamined disappointments and isolation from friendship with others. Domination and control become primary pleasures. We contract and others sense our brooding, darkening mentality. Being enslaved to this condition leaves us dead inside; an empty tomblike aura pervades in which heaviness and absence of humour are evident to all around. The need to attack others, through words or weapons, becomes part of our daily life. The output of negativity, cynicism and plotting for revenge blocks the possibility for insight into our situations.

A tendency develops to exaggerate circumstances, and this twists the truth into expediency. Facts become irrelevant or serve no other function than to be used when agreeable and suppressed when disagreeable. Such selective information perverts the truth and subjects the listener, reader or viewer to a fiction presented through a seemingly objective source of information. The perpetuation of deceptions and lies becomes the norm. There is little regard for feelings and intentions in presenting so-called objective information.

The military government, engaged in a war against terrorists, revealed to the press each day the number of terrorists killed in skirmishes. Terrorists are all those who failed to submit to the demands of the government and military. The count includes women and children.

The tobacco corporation revealed to shareholders that its worldwide sales of cigarettes had increased over the year. The company failed to report that it increased tar and nicotine content of cigarettes sold in the Third World to ensure quicker addiction.

The government claimed victory over inflation by saying that it had reduced inflation from 20% to 5%. The same government took office when inflation was less than nine per cent, lower than the average of its industrial neighbours and going down steadily.

Withdrawal from others can threaten their welfare. This can be a form of revenge and intimidation if the intention is to inflict pain or hardship. The "us" and "them" dualism thus tightens its grip over circumstances. Such threats may mask our own unresolved hurt feelings. We are unable to handle the actions or situation of others. We cannot accept the conditions triggering their actions. We want revenge. We conspire to use the same emotional strategy. "You have hurt me, so I will hurt you. The more you hurt me the more I will hurt you." A fear of punishment may inhibit this desire to hurt others, but what truly stops harmful action is insight into ourselves and events. When we feel hurt and angry, we may withdraw into sullen depression. Fearing the consequences, we may not intentionally seek revenge, but repressing the desire to harm others does not resolve the violation of human relationships.

We become trapped behind defensive barriers, which impede affection. The "us and them" dualism supports fear and desire and yields suffering. We forget the power of wise friendship, and that there are ways to respond to events which are skilful and free from aggression. Rather than dwelling on faults we can explore within ourselves and others the potential for change that is creative and challenging. Transforming our perceptions of even the most dire events is possible; when Truth emerges hostility and revenge lose their momentum. Others may still cheat and deceive us but we are wise and fearless to the ways of mental activities. We become aware of the motives of ego, and are not afraid to express concern. And when we treat others as we would have them treat us we will have finally laid to rest the "us and them" duality.

CHAPTER FIFTEEN

THE INTERDEPENDENCE OF RELATIONSHIPS

In the last century a village of nomadic North American Indians had camped for the night when a horse dealer from the nearby town of white settlers arrived. He approached the American Indian who took care of the horses and asked him how many he owned. The village man looked at him in complete puzzlement. He said that he had no idea. "The animals were just horsing," he explained. The American Indian had never thought to separate one horse from another, or to count them up.

We live in a different society with our narrow perceptions and confined sense of purpose. Individual value matters to us. We believe that the items we use are more significant if we own them. The more we own the better off we feel. We do not understand the *horsing* relationship to life. What matters is expanding the value and number of our possessions. When we view the environment as consumers and owners we only perceive profit. Unlike the North American Indian who regards himself as a "care-taker" with the horses, we have become possessors converting horses into a highly marketable commodity.

We do not understand the way we exist in relationship to our environment, and need a dramatic shift in consciousness to realize the Emptiness of a possessive relationship to things. This insight helps us to perceive the correlation between events and appreciate the mutual support system for phenomena. The possessive self clings onto objects as if that were the only form of relationship possible. The effect is a lost opportunity to explore the nature of relationship to others and the Earth.

Self-centred actions often lead to unsatisfactory results, yet our life revolves around them. Once we begin to observe the character of narrow self interest in daily life we become aware of the various underlying motives and addictions that support it. We wish to expand life's potential through pursuits in the material world, not understanding that an expansive life comes through letting go of consumer values. The desire for more things reveals an unrelatedness to the world. The pursuit and securing of the measurable and transitory neglects the aspiration and spiritual passion for the Immeasurable and Vast. As much as self is a product of the world, the world is a product of self; but only thinking makes it so. Life is a vast web of unfolding processes expressed as relationships. Refuting notions of a separate self existence, we explore life as a network of processes. Nothing and nobody have any existence outside of this relationship. When possessions do not possess our life there is the opportunity to realize an expansive vision.

Discerning individual horses and horse owner hides the web of relationships—the presence of horsing. We are reborn as horse dealers trapped in the marketplace comparing the amount others have with what we have. Self never has enough. Seeing through the phenomenon of owner and owned explodes the myth of possessions. Ultimately we have never owned anything. Everything belongs to the nature of things. Unable to stop selfish desire we perpetuate a restrictive existence. Only in despair do we have second thoughts, but our wretched involvement in desire brings us back into action through the force of conditioning. Insight and vision dissolve the narrow mind.

Personal success is the breeding ground for further desire and ambition and embraces the additional pleasures of control, self assertion, feeling superior and satisfaction in observing the failings of others. Conventional education can fulfil the expectations we and society place upon ourselves. Successful learning through passing examinations matters far more than the process of learning. To learn from experiences is to grow as a human being but conventional learning is measured through reward. Competition, the desire to do better than others or surpass a previous record, acts as an accelerator. We also learn to achieve social and financial status.

When we view a particular action as successful we repeat it.

When we fail we are adverse to repeating it. Conditioned responses, born of infatuation with goals, condition enthusiasm to learn. Learning can become nothing more than a mechanical response to the demands of society. Such activity may appear purposeful and satisfying to those who demand achievement but competitive learning distorts personality. Superiority, arrogance and pride may be the fruits of "success" while inferiority, disappointment and envy may be the fruits of "failure."

If a particular form of learning is successful, we easily take it up as a model—a fixed way of doing things so that we resist finding other ways. Thus attachment to the results of learning holds more significance than the learning process itself, even though the process is the real learning. Goal-focused learning ignores the potential to develop in a noncompetitive, non-goal-oriented way. Infatuated with tangible fruits for our efforts, we undermine the process we participate in, and the constant effort to prove our self-worth affirms our lack of it.

A conscious person interested in the web of relationships takes a real interest in the interrelationship of events. If we observe and participate instead of being spellbound with pursuit and possession, we see that motivation for personal gratification reinforces the notion of "self." Inner wisdom is not necessarily granted to those of religious persuasion or those with scientific minds—the movement and consequences of our inner life cannot be confined to ritualistic activity or empiricism. There needs to be continuity of awareness and mindfulness around knowledge and goals for the presence of wisdom to arise.

Some psychologists in a laboratory starved a cat of food. The cat could see food that was placed on one side of the hatch. Each time the starving cat approached the food, the hatch prevented it from eating. The cat clawed, bit and scratched at the hatch desperate to eat. Eventually, the paw of the cat pressed a button to enable it to go through the grill to reach the food. The experimenters starved the cat again and again to see how long the cat took to learn to press the button. The animal experimenters found out that the cat learned to find the button in an erratic way. Such experiments are irrelevant to knowledge about human behaviour, except to expose the pathological behaviour of certain scientists addicted to knowledge.

Observing the actions of "self" requires living mindfully, and a willingness to investigate the driving forces behind self interest. Investigating the scaffolding of "self" provides a host of startling insights. Our inner life comprises of moment to moment mental formations, often perceived as the effect of previous events or the cause for future effects. Through perceiving cause and effect, through interpreting the mind in such a specialized way, we become bound to time. Time, mind and the constructed self are bound together. Spiritual awakening liberates us from this psychological imprisonment, and allows us to realize the ultimate benediction.

When we refer to "the self" we think we refer to something independent, not realising that "self" is simply another mental formation. If "self" is nothing more than an abstraction from Totality then "no-self" is also. Both are equally empty of objective existence. Neither refers to any "thing." In conventional perception the "past" refers to old events instead of circulating images and associations in the Here and Now. The "self" established the "past," as a reference for the "present." Time exists through mental formations and language. To reach a goal we say we need time. Time gains a reality through the perception that a desirable end ultimately matters. We forget that time has no existence other than what self constructs for its own purposes. Conventionally it is appropriate to use concepts of time and self, but we go too far when we imagine that time and self are ultimately the way things are.

To form fixed conclusions about self and time gives them ultimate significance instead of appreciating that both concepts are a conventional agreement. Habitual conclusions about self and time inhibit awakening. Conclusions are the effect of the past masquerading in the present. They come to define the nature of the present. So conventional, unawakened existence goes on. Awakening is not separate from conventional truths, but belongs to an active expression of an Immeasurable Process. Ultimately, the affairs of the mind do not belong to ourselves but to the vast process of things. Those who have awakened to this Ultimate Truth show a responsible awareness for life, unlike those who imagine they are responsible for their lives. Tired of running alongside the force of desire and tired of running away from fears, the scaffolding of the ego loses its structure and its alleged uniqueness. Ultimately, the idea of a self having a mind in control is a fallacy, a cosmic confidence trick, an unsurpassable myth.

To believe that what we think and do does not make a difference to circumstances is the belief of someone who has not bothered to notice the movement of inner and outer life and its consequences. Our inner life is intimately involved in the world it experiences. The stars would fall out of the skies if mind existed separately from the nature of things. We have the capacity to free ourselves from cherishing the belief in time, self and mind so that action can become free from glorification of the ego.

Through sheer force of repetition, impressions seep their way into consciousness where they affect people and environment. It is not the repetition of ideas that is bad for consciousness, it is the quality of the idea and our relationship to it. To resist all harmful ideas curtails an expansive awareness, and a receptive human being welcomes exposure to ideas and insights beyond personal and national considerations.

There are ideas and concerns which we wish would take root in the collective psyche. Even when interactions seem dull and unimaginative, ideas continue to wield influence. Consciousness is sometimes like a sponge soaking up ideas whether we are aware of them or not. Being aware of what is happening makes all the difference. The ability to observe the impact of an idea provides us with options about expressing it. Wisdom perceives what is worth cultivating and what is worth letting go of.

Without awareness we become clones of a society that cherishes central ideas based on the rule of self interest. Antipathy towards those who refuse to conform to these central ideas is common; those upholding the idea that the individual rules supreme find it necessary to relegate other views to the fringes of society. To respond with love to our relationship with others, animals and environment is an act of wisdom not conditioned ideas. The inflow of new ideas challenges the influence of the old ones producing debate about the Earth and its existence, but compassionate action must follow.

The central debate is between those who champion self-interest and national interest and those whose interest is codependent relationship. Yet the buzz generated by the propagation of an idea may become addictive. Self zooms into the picture by identifying with it. Ultimate Truth remains hidden when self becomes embedded in a new paradigm, no matter how noble and insightful. Talking about "the world" becomes an intellectual competition in which promoting the paradigm takes precedence. A clever mind cannot be a substitute for wise action. The intellectual satisfaction from promoting ideas can come to matter more than anything else. The mind blinds us until there is nothing much left to applaud except accessibility to a wide range of ideas. Articulate writers and speakers achieve a reputation. There is comfort and security in avant-garde, post modern or global ideas. The satisfaction of the successful self acts like a curtain to a genuine connection with all things. What is That before the mind thinks? Ultimate Truth, unbound by any paradigm, embraces all ways of conceiving.

The notion of doing good and not doing harm becomes the predominant idea upon which existence revolves. People are either on the right side, wrong side or in need of education. The crusade to save the world is launched to reach the unbelievers and the uneducated. This will continue through the sustained view that the world needs to be saved, changed or preserved for future generations. Our ideas invite conflict or passivity. We indulge in projections and speculations about tomorrow. Letting go into the Here-Now and the response to its unfolding safeguards us from becoming lost in projections about "what might be if we continue like this." Fear of what might happen has never been much of a motivator for people to change. The future, another circulating thought, is an infinite distance away.

Sustained contact with sources of spiritual wisdom offers the possibility for realization of an interdependent understanding and action. Sources include contact with spiritual teachers, residing in a spiritual community, spending time in a sustainable culture, going into retreat or experiencing a meditative life in nature. Periods of reflective solitude also can act as a catalyst on consciousness. We start to feel kindly towards the world. We share our insights and realizations gained from our exploration into the nature of things. Regular entry into a supportive environment followed by returning to face the challenges in a suffering world is a sign of wisdom at work. The hope is that others will follow suit. Intimacy with the Here and Now commands authority and this enables responses to register directly and unambiguously. Actions are born from understanding not from self. Doing good, an idea that self fixes on, is redundant.

Those who love ideas, who wallow in them and indoctrinate others into them through the power of persuasive speech and writings will tend to be working at a distance from intimacy. Objectifiers of the world become bound to ideas. First they focus exclusively on the idea and then promote it. Of such stuff are dreams made. For example, the environment can never become a convenient appendix to our ideas. If we are dragging the environment and other issues along with us we may find ourselves suddenly stopping in midtrack. Awakening reveals the harsh truth that waving the flag of beliefs feeds conflict and abuse and does not cure global ills. When we cling to our analysis of life we construe a divided world and act from that division. The intensity of the idea only reveals that the idea has become intense. Understanding the consequences of ideas leave a vast space for the Ultimate to be revealed as a daily experience.

If we proselytize about people and environment like religious missionaries the notion of doing good produces a mixture of insights, egotism and disappointment. We may then spend the rest of our life perpetuating the insights discovered through one or two experiences. The original experience becomes an irrelevant event with intense sensations around our ideas acting as a substitute. Ideas, even the best, applied to suffering and the cessation of suffering, can overshadow enlightened intimacy with the nature of things. Wrestling with each other's ideas then takes precedence over communion with Intimacy.

Quashing others' ideas and championing our own becomes a major satisfaction. Being overworked, overcommitted, stressed out and burdened with knowledge leaves us little chance for discovering fresh waves of realization. We do not understand the suffering and happiness around us. We do not feel the grass under our bare feet, the wind no longer touches our cheeks, and our heart no longer pounds at the sight of an owl gliding across one of the remaining meadows. The dismissal of wonder and silence for conceptual reference points becomes the final act of decadence. We live our life like actors on the world stage caring only for the script. Spiritual awakening is regarded as something alien.

We ignore unintentionally one significant fact—that we are as much the environment as the earth, rivers, stars, animals and children. Organic life functions through moment to moment intimacy. Appropriate diet, regular exercise, mindfulness, respect and wisdom sustain this experience. The difference between neglect and abuse is minimal, as both reveal a desensitized relationship. We find it difficult to realize that infatuation with ideas perpetuates an alienated world. Then we are unable to express practical directions for day to day existence and our world becomes a cerebral event. Our exposure to Intimacy with the miracle of the Here and Now supplants a wealth of concepts and possessions. As the gracious American Indian revealed: "The animals were just 'horsing'". He had never thought to count them. We abide effortlessly immersed in our environment. Such experiences honour the dynamic interdependence of relationships.

Part Four
Awareness and Insight

CHAPTER SIXTEEN

IN PURSUIT OF THE SPIRITUAL EXPERIENCE

Awareness includes the precious capacity to look into the activities of our inner environment enabling us to investigate the condition of our emotional and mental life as it unfolds. The Here and Now offers an unparalleled opportunity to witness the construction of personality. We may find out some home truths, acknowledge current preoccupations and experience meditative depths. Others can support this inner inquiry. On the spiritual path, contact with like-minded people has a special place. We have the opportunity to share our experiences, look deeply together into our relationship to life and expand our understanding of spiritual teachings. This allows us to work through confusion and doubt, form deep friendships and open up our consciousness to visionary insights and actions.

The ego, however, generates difficulties. Spiritual knowledge and activities can play on notions of superiority or inferiority, we play ego games when we compare spiritual practices with others. Spiritual exploration supports breaking away from our social environment into the unknown. To keep our spirit alive and vital in the face of daily life is a challenge. The spiritual life offers the opportunity to tap into the wellspring of mystical experiences. Meditation, communication, rituals, nature, reflection and solitude all endorse the wonder of a transforming consciousness. If we develop a sense of presence in the immediate event with full and effortless attention, then we may find mystical experiences, like being born again as an adult, seeing life for the first time.

Forms include rituals, services, methods, techniques and

observations of religious rules. Formless experiences include deep meditation, palpable spiritual silences, talks on spirituality and inquiry with the wise. Spiritual forms and formlessness make their impact on consciousness. These can all be authentic expressions of ultimate wisdom. Yet they often lose their original blessing, or become the flavour of the year. We conform to the pattern until another form stimulates us.

However, clinging to spiritual forms provides security rather than awareness of what is mystical. Indulging in a particular religious belief, we cherish a form of language and ritualistic behaviour until our mind conforms to its dictates. Each new form adds colour and sparkle—imagination and initiative enliven stagnant situations. We come to believe the solution is changing or updating the forms, but as time goes by even this enlivening seems to lose its spark. The limitations of new forms can act to stultify the spiritual life as much as awaken the deep intimations of our hearts. Form and formless experiences are servants of spiritual awakening.

Moving from the known to the unknown is not an unconditional abandonment of all that we acknowledge, but includes relinquishing attachment to secular and religious forms. As worshippers we often become bound to the worshipped. The worshipped is worthy of worship not for possessing any inherent value but owing to what is invoked in the Totality of the situation. In ending identification with the worshipped the worshipper loses all meaning, all sense of significance. There are only two possibilities: either our spiritual experiences end or we explore a new sense of the spiritual life.

We may go to a church, a retreat or evening gathering with nothing much more than a wish to receive some satisfaction. There may be no genuine desire to become heartfully aware, touch depths of love or transform a narrow life. If we employ these spiritual gatherings for pleasant sensations, we have forgotten what spiritual life is. We become so used to religious forms we cannot contemplate moving outside them, and in time these vehicles for awakening become comfortable prisons.

The known and the unknown are mutually dependent. The unknown becomes the known and the known becomes the unknown. Time and changing circumstances bind the two. The unknown becomes the future, that dimension full of potential and possibilities. But the future is also known since it will consist only of a movement of the contents of consciousness. We are prone to making an enormous fuss about the known and the unknown, juggling our thoughts between the two. Never resolving our preferences we experience the dilemma of choice. We associate living with the known as desire to be secure, content and fixed in our ways. At times we abide with the known and the familiar and our life organizes itself around a regular routine. Yet this safe world has no enduring quality, as it cannot be relied on to be the same way tomorrow. The known and the secure can split asunder without a moment's notice. We may deliberately leave behind the known, or suddenly be cast into the unknown. In either case the unknown has dawned and we have to face the challenge.

When we think our life is adventurous and imaginative we may look down upon those who prefer to stay with the known, who prefer a quiet, systematic way of life. Or if our life shows years of routine we may scorn others who prefer change and movement. When we are too lazy to make the effort to understand people, we condemn them for their way of living. We think we know what is good for others, especially those who are close to us. But neither the known nor the unknown is the place to hang the hat of consciousness. Nor is there anywhere else.

Preoccupation with the known or the unknown comes through repeated emphasis. We may never feel any contentment with the known and so we lust after other things. To be with the unknown often exposes vulnerability and insecurity. We may equate the unknown with some absolute and desirable state. Or we become prisoners of the known and never risk the challenge for something greater. Exalting one over the other becomes a conditioned pattern. We dwell in the "if only" mind, and to use a well-worn cliché, the grass appears greener on the other side of the fence. The significance we give to our circumstances influences the way we think about the situation. We easily discredit or elevate our past, present and future.

In spiritual terms, we come to define ourselves through our relationship to such concepts as Enlightenment, Truth or God. One day we are far from the Truth. The next day we are close to the Truth. The third day we have found the Truth. On the fourth day we experience doubts. We fall back on spiritual concepts to measure ourselves from a spiritual perspective. Realizing the emptiness of such labels, we become liberated from any form of measurement.

We need to exercise a wise caution about defining ourselves in terms of spiritual attainments. We are likely to find ourselves mixing with those who believe us and judging those who do not. We attack others or become defensive when our statements about our attainments are challenged. Yet we cannot avoid reference points whenever we communicate. Wise attention to what we say about ourselves protects the truth of our experiences. When we start speaking about our experiences in the language of one spiritual tradition we might find ourselves ostracized by other traditions and schools. They have their language; we have our language. Various traditions imagine they are describing experiences different from each other. Identification with one tradition means agreeing to speak the same language, but holding onto one form of language hinders us from understanding the language of other religious traditions. Each time we speak we are using a language considered preferable to other ways of speaking. We can discuss, debate, agree or disagree but we will still be caught in the flow of words about words. Dropping one set of words for another may well bring pleasure or pain, please or displease our peers and impress or depress our teachers or friends.

Some spiritual traditions speak of going beyond thought. We desire to find the realm that thought cannot enter. Ironically, thought proclaims that realm. After trying to experience no-thought, we announce, quietly or publicly, according to ego needs, what we have found. The more we repeat the experience of thought proclaiming the "cessation of thought" the more likely we are to become entrenched in a belief system.

We may regard spiritual teachings as the way to the Great Unknown, like the finger pointing to the Moon. We point out the Moon rather than the finger. We think the Moon exists exclusive of the finger. We feel disturbed with the perception that the Moon only exists when the finger makes it the reference point. Spiritual teachers, whether belonging to a tradition or not, play a part in establishing both moon and finger. We pinpoint spiritual teachings as the finger, or the Moon, or both. In realization neither the moon nor finger are cherished.

Spiritual teachers may not want their followers to be liberated, for this would mean the teacher is no longer relevant to his or her disciples' spiritual awakening. The spiritually awakened no longer look up to the experiences and interpretations of another. The need for a mystical experience dissolves, and the vastness of the nature of things reveals the fiction of isolated experiences. The distinction or sameness of experiences is the play of the conventional world, the quest for experiences can be a distraction from insights and realizations. Nothing is ever the same. Nothing is ever different.

Living with a nonclinging understanding is the mark of wisdom. Not elevating our beliefs or experiences into a realm of specialness is an ongoing challenge that allows for the embrace of the known and the unknown. The imagined divisions between past, present and future lose their appearance of independent reality. It is a tragedy when the spiritual life is reduced to the decadence of claiming isolated experiences. Realizing this, we have nothing to take up, no language to limit us, nowhere to go and nobody to lead us. Reliance on others, or ourselves, fixes us into a position in the known. Others may be an inspiration to explore the mystery of things, but dependency on beliefs is no substitute for liberation.

Emptiness must be the dwelling place of those who offer spiritual teachings to others. Though we may speak with conviction, we are often only affirming the strength of language. The Truth is we believe what we say, but Truth is not a possession, nor a metaphysic, nor something of itself. We also believe those who speak the Truth like us and disbelieve those who speak the Truth differently. Our lifestyles may be similar or dissimilar but what counts is what is said. Ultimately, what truly counts goes forever unspoken.

Starting a speech by saying: "I believe that ..." instead of "The truth is ..." may leave the door open to acknowledging the beliefs of others. But the most absurd belief of all is to proclaim that we alone have the Truth and others are misguided. Much time and effort can go towards discrediting others, getting others to conform to our views and repeating ourselves incessantly. These efforts of the dualistic mind are based on the notion that if we speak loudly enough, long enough and persuasively enough we shall rally others to our cause. Those unable to stomach the Truth of the dogmatic mind announce Truth is everywhere, in everything with many paths to Truth. The ego of the narrow mind becomes the ego of the broad mind; the sweeping generalizations of support for all spiritual positions is superficial and abstract.

To pressure others to change or convert is to spread the shadow of spirituality. To realize the Emptiness of self existence negates this zeal to persuade others to believe. Not stuck in one position, consciousness has nothing to grasp onto. There is no wish to lead others up the garden path. There is instead a wise act of kindness; it is the deep heart felt wish to free others from dogma. When our heart is released from the conventional world and from religious dogma, we feel friendship for the ordinary events of life and an emancipated awareness.

Liberated from dogma our views, whether religious, social or political, express the deep intimations of our inner life. Rigidity around fixed ideas ceases so brain activity quietens and we experience a receptivity that knows no boundaries. We are no longer stuck with the known nor in pursuit of the unknown. There are no words worth clinging on to. We regard the cloud of knowing and unknowing as having no ultimate significance. Sensations and language, feelings and perceptions express the diverse field of relationships. We realize that the ending of perception and feelings is the ending of measurement, and we cannot rely upon the known or the unknown for an answer to our explorations. Neither is there anywhere else where we can go. Clouds have no ultimate power to hide the sun.

Life is not a drama that we have to work through, and death is not really the ending of the known. Yet this deception appears to give reality to the differences of life and death as independent events. Our liberation is not expressed through speaking about our so-called private world of inner silences and sensations, but through realizing the Truth in the interdependent nature of things. Ultimately, there is nothing private nor public about ourselves, and we have no life and no death.

The Ordinary and the Everyday

With the movement of thoughts and events
Separation increases and strengthens,
The frequency and continuity of movement
Solidifies our belief
Of being in conflict with life,
And all this is taken for granted.

Then one day we look outside,
Open our eyes, look around
And for a moment we sense
The possible, the probable, the actual;
The petty trivial mind
With its preoccupations and wants,
The "I" "me" and "mine" cease to function
Despite the madness, the confusion, the fear —
Another dimension briefly reveals itself.
In seeing—What utter joy!
The small mind becomes transparent, empty,
Without foundation.

Yet how easily we identify and label
Such an experience as "ultimate"
So this nondual freedom remains elusive
And we are left grasping after the ephemeral.

With no experience to hold onto,
There is no experience to lose,
Or pursue,
So why look beyond
The ordinary and the everyday?

CHAPTER SEVENTEEN

PLEASURE AND HAPPINESS

Are we happy? We have extended and stretched ourselves in many directions. Does happiness still elude us? Does this mysterious quality, in front of whose altar we genuflect, keep itself hidden? The state of happiness is not easily accessible; we can neither objectify nor purchase it. No amount of knee-bending, prayer-full activities seems to offer a happy and contented life. Yet happiness is a birthright.

We wonder why we are not happy. Perhaps the notion that the world must provide us with happiness overshadows the everyday truths of life. Getting what we want, despite the cost, often matters more than a genuine state of joy. We have become beggars at the doors of the senses. We think that tackling the world and staking our position will make us happy. We imagine that we evolve towards happiness through plundering the world. Life is neither long nor short, and it does not bestow enchantment on us all. At times we imagine we have done nothing to deserve happiness, and this may be an accurate perception. It is futile reaching out to find a jubilant existence, particularly by making endless demands on others or ourselves.

No happiness is to be found in the world.
The world does not exist to make us happy.
Happiness does not exist in anything out there.
Nor does it exist as something to be found hidden within.
Yet happiness manifests.

If we were to reflect on the mystery of happiness, it might affect our attitudes and behaviour. We would be in the process of waking up. Sleep walking through life pursuing one thing after another is abiding with indifference. Acquisitions do not make us happy. Pleasure becomes confused with happiness when, really, they are worlds apart. Pleasure is getting what we want. The stronger the desire for something or someone the greater the pleasure in success. But there is no assurance for happiness. After a long pursuit of the desirable, the resulting sensation may be flat. Pleasurable sensations often relate to the stress and tension involved in desire. "I really want to be with him or her. I really want that contact. Nothing matters as much to me in the whole world. I want to spend my life with that person. I can't think about anything else."

We confuse happiness with the experience of relief in uniting with the person or situation of our dreams. Securing a relationship that we pursue generates a mass of satisfied sensations. "We are together. I have never been so happy in my whole life. I can't tell you the joy this person brings me. I'm happy beyond my wildest dreams." When we hear such statements we tend to squirm. An instinct tells us that the intensity of this person's pleasure is going to change; the person will have difficulty in coping with the change or will mindlessly carry on doting upon the other person, ignoring all change as long as possible.

We repeatedly confuse happiness with the end of desire. The desire for another, goods or status is a burden. We believe we can only free ourselves from this burden of desire through succeeding in our pursuits. This goes a step further with the false assumption that the more we succeed the greater the happiness. Yet where is the evidence? The idolatrous worship of people and objects becomes a refuge in which to hide our empty existence. We lose ourselves in the world of pleasure and pain. We think we are astute and intelligent through knowing what we want and going for it, gut we aren't happy.

Thus pleasure is relieving desire, often artificially created and nurtured by social conditioning. Relief from desire becomes the main drive for being alive. Competing for particular desires constitutes the bulk of daily life activities; common desires hold countless numbers together. The cost to people, animals and the Earth's limited resources becomes irrelevant; the pursuit of pleasure suffocates the passion for awakening to Immensity. To take a gross example: the fox-hunters get their pleasure from the hunt and satisfaction from the kill. The hounding to death of a fox is a legal activity which the fox-hunters have developed to support their pursuit of pleasure. They disregard the value of humane relationships between humans and animals, and the fox cubs left to starve to death. So the sport, the logic and the pleasure continue. It's the pleasure that finally counts. Our society shares the mentality of the fox-hunter—as little as possible must interfere with our pleasure seeking.

Television viewers derive interest and pleasure from only a small number of the programmes viewed; many programmes neither inform nor entertain. Contact with a screen of dots spellbinds consciousness in an escape from the desire-stress-goal mode. We cannot influence the next sequence of dots on the channel. The only choice is to change channels or switch off. The end of viewing lies out of our hands, unless we break the spell by switching the television off. Thus we are relieved from thinking everything has to be under our control. Owing to the degree of hypnosis involved in television and video viewing we may not have the power to apply the off switch even if bored. To turn off requires awareness and an effort to reach the remote control or pull ourselves out of the armchair. No wonder the average number of hours each person watches television a week is equal to three full working days.

Involvement in new and creative activities generates happiness and pleasure. Consciousness, stimulated by the new, finds fresh levels of energy with the unfamiliar. When we remain fresh and receptive to the creative and spiritual in the Here and Now, we access contentment. When the stimulating becomes an ordinary event with the familiarity of brushing of teeth, we become habitual.

We know happiness cannot be bought—something we often comment on in our philosophical moments. We spout such words of wisdom with a confidence that is alarming, as our values and activities reveal immense self-deception. We speak such truths with an impressive voice of authority, yet we live in another way. We *act* as though happiness can be bought or earned through accumulated efforts, a combination of knowledge, energy, hard work and luck. But this is not the vehicle for happiness. It is only the road to the relief of desire and achievement of transitory pleasure.

We pit ourselves against the world. Our obdurate mind fastens onto things with an impatient grasping that seems implacable.

The tyrant and the plunderer never seem far from consciousness, and deep in this devilish mind lies self interest. This view of life subjugates as many circumstances as possible to the interests of the ego. Our delusion truly manifests in the self-righteous proclamation that we live in the real world. Being pragmatic and straightforward becomes a way of life for the self-serving and the unashamedly insensitive.

We trade off pleasure and disappointment at the expense of enchantment and wonder with the unfolding nature of the Here and Now. We never seem to understand that the mystery of happiness lies in intrinsic intimacy with an expansive life. Happiness is not approachable nor accessible; no amount of effort and knowledge will entice it. Unlike the sensation of pleasure, it is not an offshoot from gaining a hold over the desirable. Happiness does not exist by itself nor as a by product of fulfilled desires. We have to put aside the mind preoccupied with desire, action and result and start participating in the world without that three fold involvement being our raison d'être. The sublime sweetness of life exists in interaction, with a delight not tied to wanting and possessing, nor dependent upon anything for its presence.

Happiness is indefinable. It comes unexpectedly—in moments of quietude and spontaneous receptivity. An inconsequential event can grace our lives with awe and bliss. There is no working hard for such an experience. There is no capacity to possess such an event and repeat it at will. Not driven by desire nor held back with fear, we become receptive to daily benedictions that place our activities and the results from them in a proper perspective.

Putting aside this cruel pretence
Of civilization amid our broken toys
Let us go and hover in the mellow mist.
Stillness nourishes our deepest recesses;
The nightingale fills the dark's hollow;
We kneel upon the Earth with naked hands.
Long grass bends kindly underneath us.
On this day we utter a silent prayer
That pays respect to the song of the Earth.

Poets and artists have attempted to convey the intimations of enchantment, to ground its mystery in the fabric of everyday existence. Happiness is a response to the vast symphony of Immediacy. The addictions of self-centred activity incarcerate the self so that we are unable to touch the untrammelled beatitude of the Extra-ordinary. In letting go of the compulsive quest for pleasure we risk being happy.

Recognizing the futility of bondage to goals, wisdom bursts the bubble of our mediocre self, bent on gratification. Not slavishly following whims for this or that is a liberating process. The mind's desires cannot orchestrate That which is vast. The humility of Here and Now mindfulness exposes the potential for a wondrous sense of aliveness allowing an expansive witness of timeless presence. Both the whole and the part embrace a joyful perception. When we see that our whims cannot orchestrate existence, we dwell in a joyful and enigmatic presence. When desire, action and result are relieved from the pressure of ego investment, they take their appropriate but not exaggerated place in the immeasurable sanctity of universal belonging.

We fear that if we do not pursue self interest others who are ambitious and competitive will walk over us. We believe the world is rough and everyone is in it for themselves. It is no easy undertaking to question the social conspiracy that keeps us imprisoned in such fears. However, to imagine that letting go of the pleasure hunt automatically entitles us to happiness is still imprisonment to cause and effect. Joyful revelations are not available through subversion of the will, nor through the marketplace mentality of trading one thing for another. We cannot walk into a vast field of wonder just by stepping out of the old. Happiness is not the reward of a benevolent universe for sacrificing old ways of behaving. We have to take risks and forget our fears.

In abandonment, we prepare ourselves for what we cannot comprehend; yet striving to understand sublime feelings violates them. Whatever we do to understand the mystery of genuine happiness we come unstuck. Our efforts to comprehend it are inconsequential, and our determination to find happiness is the surest way to guarantee that it will remain elusive. Its mystery reveals the interaction of heart, mind, senses and world and knows no formula. This elusive state, subtle and insubstantial, defies knowledge, willpower and religious beliefs.

The joyful communicate a peace with themselves, their environment and with the unfolding of life. They see through the dualities of conflict and demand and iron-fisted methods to get their own way. The unfathomable experience of happiness brings spontaneous contentment, and this joy transcends reason and words. This is a celebration amidst our tortured world, but we do not know where these peak experiences come from and where they go. In conversation we attribute our happiness to a certain set of circumstances, but deep down we know this is not the case. The same circumstances can be repeated without our feeling any special happiness at all.

We experience mystery. Abiding in a world full of intrigue, we realize paradoxical situation about happiness leaves us baffled. It is as if we are forever telling ourselves what we should do to solve our problems and concerns; yet this very effort easily perpetuates them. We seem doomed to repeat history. The action of going for what we think we want ensures the denial of what we really want. In the end, we must bow down to the enigmatic expression of existence. In this spirit, daily events touch the depths of being. Intuition gladdens our questioning heart by intimating there is no fixed solution. There is no personal power to produce joy; it remains elusive quite apart from the demands of self interest.

This moment suddenly stands still
Like it never was before,
Spreading out before the eyes,
Filling the region of other times.
What remains is forever unplanned.

How fortunate it is that the same miraculous events of inter action do not produce the same reaction in all of us. If that were possible we would be bound to a mechanical, inorganic universe with nauseating predictability. We might then believe that time and place cause happiness. Who would want to make happiness a watertight experience, a predictable event to be turned on and off at will? For it is wonderful to live without assurance. Lightness, playfulness and jubilant participation in the Symphony of life may not suffuse us each moment, but not to be touched spontaneously with joy, not to experience daily this ungovernable happiness, is an incomparable loss.

We may be blessed to come across others who live differently, whose presence brings joy and sanity. What does such a person see? What enables that person to respond effortlessly and joyfully to that others ignore? There is benefit from communicating with such people, as some of their insights may rub off. Happy people may try to describe their attitudes, their relationship to the world, and their realizations. Yet their description cannot provide answers, no matter how precise or poetic such people are. Language does not add or subtract one iota from the quality of happiness; words are neither inside nor outside contentment.

This sublime stuff called happiness is never more than a moment away, an indescribable contact with the majesty of existence. As a palpable presence, its revelation remains ungraspable and unretainable while suffusing those people beyond desire. Its enchanting touch dissolves the boundaries between the domestic and the divine. The Vast Symphony of life pervades our being with a light that cannot be extinguished.

CHAPTER EIGHTEEN

A MOMENT OF INSIGHT

At times, it seems the light of Truth calls us. If so, we have the right to abandon our children, our partner and our home for the spiritual quest. To remain in some orderly career or household carving out an existence motivated by money and security does not lead to an imaginative spiritual awareness. Pushing our children into private education and fretting over what to buy the in-laws to keep them sedated trivializes the depths of human relationships. Values become perverse. A moment of insight might reveal an ungodly message that we spend our life in a straitjacket. How long can it go on like this? The protestations of friends and family are normal reactions to our decision to listen to spiritual yearnings, but their voices must not take priority over the spiritual quest.

Moments of insight into our circumstances occur spontaneously, through cultivating awareness and stepping back to look at how we live our lives. We may realize we are trapped in circumstances or even wasting our life. Our insights may reveal we have squandered the past and that this squandering continues into the present. Not only do we believe we are wasting our life, but can see no hope for anything different in the future. We may discover that this is an intolerable situation. But the effect of this awareness could be to leave us resigned to an ensnared life. Society provides little consolation following such a revelation, and a cursory glance into the circumstances of others shows the same sort of behaviour. It seems there is a social plot to fix people's circumstances. "You can't just run off, you know."

The actions that follow a moment of insight may trigger a chain of reactions from others. Loved ones may feel threatened, as ending one role ends roles for others, too. Accusations fly back and forth in the debate over whether an action initiated by one person is an expression of a spiritual calling or selfishness. Such issues are never as black or white as we imagine. Revolutionizing our life is not going to please all the people, all the time. It requires spirit, integrity and determination not to confuse selfishness with clarity; this is a genuine concern. Is our situation to be altered, or our relationship to it to be investigated?

The spirit of a new found independence can have an adverse affect on others, who are unable to understand the changes taking place in our life. We have a right to make a fresh start and to become fully alive. But the decision to do so may have to be followed through in the face of hostility. Yet those who cannot understand why we are changing should not be blamed. Others may not understand a life-changing decision, so we react with impatience and resentment. We stop listening and conflict ensues—whatever happened to this new found spiritual realization?

We have to look deep into ourselves to see whether such a major change is necessary and appropriate. Our actions may generate long term pain for those who are close to us and depend on us for support. We may discard the familiar on impulse only to enter a mutual back-slapping cult. We may even believe we are making spiritual progress, whereas we have only substituted one demanding family for another. Perhaps we find an unguarded moment of unattached being is unnerving, which brings a fitful uncertainty about what direction our life is going in. However it goes, it is valuable to exercise our right to discover our function, if any, in the universe.

From moments of insight we can conclude that no opportunity for worthwhile change is possible. This view often evokes retaliatory reactions in us, which we then dump onto those we are close to, blaming them for what is lacking in ourselves. We may even blame others for our personal circumstances, and berate our colleagues, friends and relatives for our own problems.

We also can berate ourselves for feeling resigned to circumstances. If blaming others is not enough, then the accusing finger turns to ourselves. The mind manufactures a litany of "if only I had" "if only I hadn't." These short-sighted views offer little in the way of understanding but much towards undermining our fragile sense of self worth. The reactive self corrupts the moment of insight; instead of being a turning point to freedom it only reveals how restrictive life is. Pressured by conventional agreement, we conform to the common will rather than seek to find our way out of the dark labyrinth. "I have no choice. I have to put up with my situation."

The deep inner yearnings for happiness and Freedom are not quashed by submission to circumstances. Latent unrest will be the constant reminder of not being and doing what we want. Others may appear content with their lot in life, and even appear to flourish in similar circumstances; perhaps they have not sensed how incongruous their life is. Or perhaps they are genuinely content with their circumstances. But the contentment of others is not a reference point for ourselves. Blaming others, or ourselves, or just circumstances hinders direct, unequivocal liberating insights.

If we renounce these copouts hindering genuine metamorphosis, we arrive at the barefaced Truth. We now have the responsibility to step out of life denying circumstances. They may not be violent and initiate exploitation but simply suffocating or soul destroying. We can initiate change. Sweeping out the old may alienate people who dislike the reorganizing of their loved one's life. Those established in a set pattern do not take kindly to the dissident touched with insight who says: "NO!" or "No more." The chance for a free life, a creative and exploratory existence is available, including concern for others, an engaged spirituality.

We may however decide to continue to work within a familiar environment, and the sense of duty that accompanies it. This is the challenge: to live an emancipated life through trust, expression of deeper values, and awareness, integrity and compassion, without necessarily making sweeping changes to our material circumstances. Money, consumer items and status are minor considerations. The refusal to remain with the old conditioning involves more than taking initiative. Those of conservative disposition are shocked at the easy adjustment of someone who abandons the old and embraces a new way of being. "Doesn't anything from the past matter?" "How can you shrug off years of commitment as if nothing ever occurred?" "What kind of person are you?"

We become attracted to the ultimate realizations of those dedicated to spiritual values. Religious texts can then be a source of comfort since they portray individuals who abandoned all for the pursuit of Truth. Realizing we have to make changes in our life if we are to taste something deeply spiritual, we either abandon our familiar world or transform our relationship to the daily realities.

Spiritual seekers who dump their social responsibilities often feel light and happy for a period. They report that they feel more alive and speak of the dramatic shift they have made in their lives for the sake of spirituality. Having put aside the familiar they absorb themselves in the spiritual realms. They are able to experience temporarily a state of abiding in the unknown, so highly prized by the mystic. Shaking off the past means a carefree flow —for a while. The unknown, bound to time, is forced to become the known. The step into the unknown loses its magic and the tide of personal history creeps into consciousness. The known before was the home, partner, job and children. Now the known has become religious forms, the company of like-minded people and a daily routine. Isn't this only shifting around the contents of consciousness?

It is however unkind to reduce a major transition in the seeker's life to nothing more than a change of mental furniture. Many are willing to make enormous sacrifices for the sake of awakening consciousness. There are seekers who listen and respond fully to their spiritual yearnings, taking bold steps in their quest for spiritual truths. Their courage has been a source of inspiration for others. A penetrating moment of insight and consequent non attachment enables us to consider our circumstances. When a person has chosen a new way of life, the old lifestyle may not seem worthy of discussion; certainly not worth continuing in. Moments of insight are not rational, and the past may be regarded as a forgettable, if not regrettable, incident.

The revolutionary leap of faith and the novelty of the new become in time old, familiar and potentially imprisoning. It is as if nothing really changed. We jumped out of one hole, enjoyed the air, and jumped straight into another one. Letting go does not guarantee Freedom unless insights into Freedom have penetrated our inner depths. The capacity to listen totally and deeply and to be free from clinging expresses spiritual wisdom.

The initial shock of awareness may not carry the depth of realization about our life that we imagined. The moment of insight may only be an explosive expression of our wish to escape from circumstances. What is the difference between running away from a situation and initiating steps into an emancipated way of life? We need to inquire into ourselves regularly to be clear about the differences. The thoughts of others, for or against, may sway our decisions, but the final understanding rests with ourselves. Is there a pattern of running away every time feelings of being trapped occur? Is there a pattern of running away when we are not receiving the degree of attention we think we deserve? The liberating vitality that major change brings is not an optimal experience, but may indicate a step in the right direction.

Awareness of Totality from an insight rather than just its particular parts is a tribute to understanding. Entering unknown territory without parents, guide, or even friends (with perhaps only a few clues from the spiritually aware) reduces the tendency to get high. Yet joy and gladness are authentic emotional responses to insights, innovating adroit and wise moves into a fresh beginning. An underlying satisfaction, a sweetness, and lightness of being are the rewards for taking these risks.

Sometimes, having undergone an honest evaluation of our circumstances, we decide we cannot walk out. Recognizing the escapist pattern we decline to walk away from our commitments. Love for our children, sickness of a loved one, or the absence of financial resources continue to shape our personal environment. Inquiry is still appropriate if we have decided to stay, as our relationship to the situation can be investigated and changes of attitude explored. Each day displays a sequence of events worthy of mindfulness and discovery. Our experiences are the raw material for learning about our feelings, thoughts and perceptions, and conscious action pays tribute to our existence. No situation is without opportunity.

Unless some re-evaluation takes place following a moment of insight we are likely to hold ideals of how it could be. Skilful change is the spearhead for awakening within a familiar context. Creative interpretation originates through observing and noting the changes needed. The spirit for change has to inform our circumstances without delay, otherwise we linger in various states of dissatisfaction and wishful thinking. The capacity to work with a situation sweetens the emotional response to it. Small changes acted upon with passion and determination can make all the difference to daily life. A human being still exercises the inalienable right to carry out change—such as changing one's attitude and implementing an awakened vision.

From a moral standpoint, a change of circumstances takes priority if activities include the direct harming or trampling over the needs of others, animals or environment. Sending loving kindness to those that we continue to harm is not enough; the activities must stop. Freedom of action is not achieving the desire to do what we like. Liberation involves consideration of moral, social and global issues, whereas the ego easily discards them. Freedom is authentic when it is expansive, genuinely considerate and not obscured by selfish desire.

When we dig deep into ourselves we find the resources to express an emancipated view of circumstances. If we cannot find these resources within, it is vital to find support from those who understand our dilemma. We may have to endure highs and lows until we become steady in the face of change. Freedom is not a metaphysical abstraction unrelated to experience. Unable to recognize an experiential liberation, we think of ourselves as conditioned creatures unable to transcend circumstances. We become alienated from our daily life and feel apart from Freedom. Instead of allowing insights we philosophize. It is the love of Freedom that enables us to say "NO" to what is unacceptable and be willing to face the consequences. Insight is the resource for significant change, whereas blind reaction makes no real difference.

We think of Freedom and the fulfilment of our spiritual life as the result of fundamental changes, but Freedom reveals itself in the beginning, middle and end of life's processes. When we separate salvation from the world we elevate it into metaphysical realms, placing Freedom in some unique category. It becomes vague, otherworldly, or exclusively a religious or philosophical belief. Regarding Freedom as something to be gained is a limited view of its ultimate significance.

We pay tribute to our profound capacity to transcend circumstances by exercising our right to break out of a mould, to give up the weight of the past, to find peace and genuine connection. This down to earth Freedom never neglects the ordinary things of life. An inspiring Truth of our daily existence is the potential for everyday occurrences to be the sources of ultimate illumination. We then accommodate the events of the universe, including birth and death. Conventional freedoms may be taken away by political, economic and social circumstances, but Ultimate Freedom remains unburdened by the passage of time, events and change.

The testimonies of enlightened women and men throughout the ages have given witness to the sovereignty of Freedom. They have regarded life as a sacred and precious event. Some have found themselves in the most tragic of circumstances, deprived of all human rights, having lost all opportunity for self expression. Yet their Freedom has remained untouched despite such vicissitudes. Others realize Freedom without such trials. Physical or environmental circumstances cannot daunt the power to realize ultimate Freedom.

The challenge of life is to set each other free from suffering and attachment. Pressure on others often only thwarts their attempts to be free. Those who face the vicissitudes of life with spiritual awareness can experience liberating insights into painful circumstances. They witness the Truth. The potency of events to oppress then dwindles away. The peace of realization goes beyond knowledge of the world, social structures and sensations. Spiritual wisdom arises like the wondrous dawn of a new day. In the Emptiness of the ego, everything falls into place. Emptiness makes all things possible.

CHAPTER NINETEEN

BEING THERE

The gardener would not dream of leaving his home, family or garden in the pursuit of some spiritual quest. He understands the nature of the Here and Now and is not caught up in the forces of leaving and arriving in the name of the spiritual search. The gardener takes care of his garden with a reverence that makes his work an act of worship. He plants his flower seeds with tender, loving care. He bends down at the flower bed fashioning the hole to plant the seeds. He pours seeds into his hand, gently and mindfully. The gardener might be a priest offering holy communion. He has ensured the ground is moist and firm. He maximizes the opportunity for the seeds to take root. On long, hot, dry days the loving gardener walks out daily to the flower bed and, with unfailing regularity, waters the ground. He acts with the quiet, confident knowledge that further life will spring forth out of the soil.

The process appears almost ritualistic to the outsider, but the gardener cherishes each moment. In a profound way seeds, plants and flowers are interrelated since they intimate wonder. They convey something greater than their initial appearance. He notices that not all the seeds became flowers even when all the conditions appeared satisfactory. Over the years, the gardener has learned not to cherish expectations—a wisdom safeguarding excessive hope.

The garden brings joy into his life. The gardener never thinks of himself as being religious; he finds church services rather boring. He prefers the aroma of flowers to that of incense. He loves the Earth so much that he has never thought to put his experience into words, even though for him it is religious. It doesn't seem necessary. Duty in life is planting seeds, caring for them, watching them grow and witnessing the fruits with a sublime appreciation of the unfolding.

His experience is a world of becoming, a kaleidoscope of diversity. Nothing remains the same, not for a moment. Events and circumstances interact with endless variations on the theme of becoming. When the gardener stops for a moment or two to contemplate the range of sentient and insentient life forms, he greets with awe the abundance of life in soil, water and air. The dynamic interplay of life imprints itself on consciousness via the senses. The impact of this world not only supports consciousness but contributes to shaping it. He realizes he belongs to this interplay so he adapts to his environment; he reflects its character, nurtures its process and addresses its needs.

The interdependence of the gardener with the garden is understood through contemplative awareness, and serves as the raw material for ultimate realization. Is the gardener shaping the environment or is the environment shaping the gardener, or both, or neither? Participating in this relationship, the gardener dwells on the revelation of his nonseparate existence. He regards any fixed view of this relationship with circumspection. To point the finger in one direction neglects the other. He sees he cannot make absolute statements about this relationship to the garden. What shapes what? The gardener's insights awaken to the touch of the ineffable. Neither self nor environment are the single cause for his experiences. Yet the Totality of things makes a tangible and indescribable impact on consciousness.

Awareness and self-knowledge include understanding the nature of this impact. How is the world affecting the state of consciousness? What does that mean in practical terms? Theories have little relevance here; they only obscure an opportunity to learn about the impact of life on life registering throughout the living organism. The world around leaves no part untouched. The gardener is the environment as much as the flower seeds in the earth. When gardeners neglect the interconnection, the dependent arising of all things, they engage in abuse. When we do not treat the Earth right, the Earth does not treat us right. There is no beginning to this relationship, no first cause, as it is an unfolding cycle of interdependency. Abuse of interdependency can be far-reaching before all hell breaks loose. Every thing, every cell pays a high cost for our belief in self existence. Ignoring the intimacy that the environment and human beings are non-different produces suffering. The benefit of awareness is the revelation of the connection of ourselves to the Earth. Humanity can either increase or decrease disasters in the world.

The gardener, engaged in mindful and concentrated activity, applies consciousness to basic life processes. He also spends many hours in the quietude of an allotment, the greenhouse and his organic vegetable plot. Teachings of the relativity of time and becoming are offered for those with eyes to see. If the conditions are there the plant will respond to the sun. No mind can list the unaccountable number of conditions required for one plant to burst open into human consciousness. Why? For a single vegetable to grow the rest of the universe, including sun, oxygen and water is necessary; they are all codependent. Whatever is unfolding in the Here and Now is a vital ingredient for the vegetable to be ready. This linked chain of conditions shows that if one particular factor were not present in the Here and Now the process would collapse. Even that would not be the case; the process of becoming would cease to exist.

The various conditions of existence make up our existence. Our cells are made up of all cells. We are as much earth, water, air, light, flowers, trees, stones, clouds and sunshine as we are human. Hands-on awareness reveals the unfolding process of arising and passing, existence and nonexistence. We do not have to be a scientist to make such discoveries. There is the continuing encounter of existence with itself. Interconnection is not apparent at first. We can explore the nature of causes and effects and how it manifests in our lives and the lives of others—like the way the gardener responds to events in the garden. In these pragmatic realizations we live wisely amid change and diversity.

To probe further into becoming is to see that we all share three characteristics: arising, staying and passing. Wherever attention turns there is an immediate example of these, either through direct experience or inference. The flame on the end of the match appears, stays for a time and passes. Human experience takes one form one day, one moment, only to become something different. No experience is permanent, and signs indicate that the world itself is not an eternal phenomenon; neither are human beings. A world of becoming is a world without constancy. Impermanence is the mark of daily life.

At times, our heart and mind rejoice in this process of becoming. At other times things are difficult, painful, frustrating. An issue refuses to go away. The longing for it to be over robs us of rest and sleep. Fretting at the possible outcome, days languish, waiting for the fateful moment, the day of judgement. The world of becoming fades into obscurity as attention wraps itself around the repetitive thoughts and feelings. "What will be the outcome of this.?" No magic wand is available, no psychic can predict the future. Nobody, divine or human, knows. It seems unfair and unjust to have to live with uncertainty. Then the news breaks out. Relief floods, saturates the cells of the organism; the mind peaks at new heights of gratitude. Impermanence is as welcome as peace.

Impermanence is not always treated with such relish. Good news becomes bad news. Success becomes failure, health becomes sickness, profit becomes loss and praise becomes blame. Becoming denies guaranteed continuity of what is good. What we deem good others may dislike. We become aware of our value judgements, and that our vested interests cannot ensure the desired results. The extreme views that events are predetermined or that through free will we can make anything happen seem incongruous. Dwelling on the diversity of becoming, we might conclude that the way things turn out is in the hands of the gods. To what degree the outcome of events is in the hands of the gardener is equally debatable. Led to believe that we can do anything we want to do and become anything we want is a cruel hoax. People, including politicians, educators and parents, play it on themselves and others, especially children.

It is in the nature of interdependent arising that we cannot all get what we want from life. In our lack of wisdom and failure to see into the processes of becoming, we often escape into a fantasy world where dreams are substituted for actuality. We imagine glory lies in controlling events. A minority get what they want, often on the backs of others. They treat single-mindedness and the competitive drive as virtues. They are blind to what they do and how it affects others.

The compulsive achiever gives immense significance to his or her pursuits. The achiever puffs up the ego instead staying in touch with the processes of change in the conventional world. The wise old proverb says that what goes up must come down. The achiever achieves and fails to achieve. His fortunes go up and down. Fear, regret and struggle belong to the endless trials to preserve that which remains impermanent. The seed which becomes a plant becomes a flower. The flower withers and fades. The gardener knows this, so he is free from worry. The achiever cannot understand why the results are different from the dream. Unimpressed with such ego centred obsessions, the gardener mindfully cultivates his garden. He remains in harmony with unfolding processes through the days, weeks and seasons. Knowing from experience that there are no guarantees of the fruits of his work, he works with humility and love. The gardener's intimacy of relationship with the immediate environment matters above all else. Deep down in his heart, he knows that taking care of today enables tomorrow to take care of itself. His wisdom lies in being in touch with the cycle of life. Being in harmony with becoming the gardener safeguards himself from triggering off endless internal polemics about "what to do next in my life." He sees that redemption lies in the ordinary and does not despair of the soil nor make demands on it. He knows that wherever he is, whatever comes to him is not different from anything else. All events share the characteristic of arising, staying and passing. He is not afraid of change, nor unexpected results.

The gardener does not regard the process of becoming as a sequence *doomed* to end in death and destruction but knows that the ending of one sequence is the seed for another. He knows it has always been like this. This quiet wisdom does not invoke decisions to avoid contributing to the arising and passing of events, even if it were possible. His contentment embraces every single aspect of the process. This wisdom is a joyful liberation, unbound to arising, staying and passing away. He understands what it means to live in the world, but not be of the world.

The wisdom of the gardener does not have to be labelled spiritual. Spiritual feelings are also subject to arising, staying and passing. He enjoys the wisdom that experiences change and nonattachment to results. Spiritual experiences become limited to particular sensations that occur in time and place. These experiences may make much or little difference to our life. Exploring life's processes offers a continual revelation. The gardener's "spirituality" liberates him from the distraction of religious beliefs. He realizes he participates in a daily miracle that expresses Immensity.

The gardener participates in the process of becoming but is not bound to it. He sees his role as gardener as a function of Totality not an identity. Intention, action and results embrace us and all existence. What is a valid intention? What will enable that intention to mature into action? What will the relationship be to the results? He knows the happiness of participation in codependent arising. He draws effortlessly from his past without feeling haunted. If the gardener thinks he can control results, he knows he is playing God. He cares for the effects of his efforts but understands that their intention, action and result belong to the process of things not to him.

He continues to care for the earth. He recognizes the potential for change due to foreseen and unforeseen circumstances and this curbs investments in results. He knows the futility of fighting the flow of becoming. He sees the present as an expression of purposeful activity in which he is participating. He does not give exaggerated value to his work for he understands that his livelihood is related to the realm of Immensity. The beauty of freedom from clinging to desired ends allows cooperation and wonder to happen simultaneously. The gardener and the garden are entrusted to each other. The gardener with his garden fork, hoe and rake lovingly sets the garden in motion. He can conceive of the future yet he does not have the power to make each plant grow to the proportions that he wants. His influence only *seems* extensive. He always remembers he is as much an interdependent part of the garden as the seeds sown. The gardener belongs to the garden. The gardener exists through the garden. The garden ceases to exist when the gardener ceases. The faux pas of perception is to take for granted the garden as independent of the gardener. Out of touch with the relationship between the perceiver and the perceived we imagine that every view we form is an expression of the way things really are. We act as if the world was completely separate from our perceptions and that the traumas and dramas of the world bear no relationship to our perception.

The gardener has seen the effects of mind, driven by ambition to control and determine events. He knows this is an extreme form of behaviour. But he has not fallen into the other extreme of alienation where events become detached from the perceiver of them. Putting the spade into the ground, turning the earth over, the gardener touches the middle way between the two extremes. He may not be able to articulate his understanding but he expresses it in the muddied boot pushing the spade into the ground.

When there is freedom from conditioned thought the gardener and garden become the revelation of something other than just the process of becoming. The Vastness of mystery is interrelated with events. While the brow sweats, the butterfly moves and rests among the flower beds, sunlight touches the petals, and the decomposing weeds in turn become food. The absolutism attributed to birth and death finds no place in the Vastness of nature. Nothing appears to be what it is and nothing appears to be otherwise.

When the gardener transcends his conditioned views of garden life, he does not believe his gardening is evolving, nor does he believe it isn't. This liberates his mind and his constructed views are unimportant. Like the garden, he is free from temporal concerns. Since the flower has no particular purpose, it touches a place of whole-hearted responsiveness deep within. The flower does not possess a notion of concept of coming from anywhere or going anywhere. Neither does the gardener.

Clinging to a particular viewpoint exposes an obdurate mind. In that realization before the mind takes formation, Immensity stands alone when the doors of perception are open. The Emptiness of things stands free from construction, concepts, definitions yet made present through the appearance of the gardener and the garden. The gardener is not the enlightened answer, nor is the garden, yet spiritual awakening is found Here and Now. When all ways of expressing have exhausted themselves, then all things have exhausted themselves; there is only That which is timeless.

Cause-effect and becoming are inseparably linked. Becoming is a valid interpretation of relative truth for human beings to experience harmony with the immediate environment. Realizing this, the gardener takes care of his garden with a reverence that makes his work an act of worship. He plants his flower seeds with tender, loving care. He bends down at the flower bed fashioning the hole to plant the seeds. He pours seeds into his hand, gently and mindfully. The gardener might be a priest offering holy communion. He has ensured that the ground is moist and firm to maximize the opportunity for the seeds to take root. On long, hot, dry days the loving gardener walks out daily to the flower bed and, with unfailing regularity, waters the ground. He acts with the quiet, confident knowledge that further life will spring forth from the soil.

CHAPTER TWENTY

REACTION AND STILLNESS

Reaction and stillness appear as opposites. We know what it is like to be caught up in a state of reaction and we know moments of quietude, a sense of sublime stillness. Our life unfolds through reaction and stillness.

Reaction

Thoughts and ideas become embedded within as centres of reaction. At times, we are compulsively attracted towards one thing and show aversion to something else. At other times, we feel grateful when we are not reacting. Reactions become a moving conglomeration of mental and emotional accumulations around a central idea. They are given substance through identification and become filters in consciousness, affecting the way we treat others and ourselves.

When our reactions operate negatively, they inhibit direct and appropriate behaviour. Reactions are unwholesome since they fuel actions that we later regret. Doing good can be the consequence of reaction as much as doing harm—doing good can be as compulsive as evil. Ending personal reactivity is the dissolution of embedded ideas of doing what is good and not good. To investigate the mutual support that "good" and "not good" give each other is to realize that one cannot be without the other. Our past conditions form these ways of relating to life.

Poverty haunted the family. An apple had to be cut into four pieces, one piece for each child, as the parents could not afford a piece of fruit for each child. Shoes were passed down from the oldest child to the youngest. Blankets and heavy clothes provided the main source of heating. Such upbringing imprints itself in the psyche. When one child grew to adulthood, she worked to improve the lot of the poor. The struggle for social justice became a lifelong battle, clearly defined for the poor and against the rich. Such a struggle fuelled her hate for the wealthy based upon childhood experiences.

Memory, feelings and investment lead to attraction and aversion stimulating reaction. Moving back and forth between these opposite reactions becomes irksome, constant polarizing intensifies love and hate. The world becomes black and white, good and bad, enlightened and unenlightened. These perceptions distort events like cracks in a mirror; the world becomes fragmented with one piece set up against another. At times this polarization causes perception to become so distorted that the wrong, the impure and the unenlightened must be dismissed or condemned for being who they are. In the same way we heap condemnation upon ourselves through identifying with a negative reaction. Insight into our "self" is often insight into personal reactivity. We reflect on what we can learn each time we mindlessly react.

Meditative awareness contains both direct experience and wise evaluation of the processes of experience. Valuing one thing *against* something else is an action of discernment, appropriate in certain situations. When this discernment is born out of a personal reaction we cling to our experience and our interpretation of it, and reject other reactions. But the unwanted and devalued must be dealt with. Such dualistic perceptions distance us from peace of mind and prevent us from understanding others.

Contentment abides beyond the pull of reactivity. Understanding and skilful action emerge from clear awareness not reaction. Insight from meditation into our reactions reduces their potency, but if we misunderstand the process of meditation, we can reinforce our reactivity. Misunderstanding meditation also can lead to suppressing feelings and thoughts in order to remain unruffled. Restricting freedom of expression often leads to feeling heavy, dull and sluggish. Although repression of thoughts and feelings gives a temporary rest from mental gymnastics, this state is not to be confused with authentic stillness.

What are the underlying motives that reinforce reactions? Am I being driven by my reactions? Directly questioning our personal reactivity to situations is often the equivalent of putting a stick in the spokes of a moving bicycle. The separation from peace can seem like an unbridgeable gulf. Letting go of investment in our reactions dissolves their blinding influence and reveals intimations of a depth of stillness immediately accessible.

Stillness
The beginner to meditation may regard stillness as a sacrifice of spontaneity, repression of feelings and denial of an expressive self. When we are constantly caught up in reactions we think this is the normal state of being. The significance of stillness is exposed through experience. A sublime interfused awareness is appreciated in the moments that it occurs. Agitation and dissatisfaction also highlights the value of stillness and contemplation. Through direct experience we can understand the value of serenity and its significance for action.

Imagine what it would be like to able to be still, utterly still. Body, emotions and thoughts would not impinge in an unsatisfactory way on consciousness. The murmurings, chatterings and incessant inner dialogues would fade away, we would register contentment right through our very cells. Each nuance, each sublime intimation of the Here and Now would be appreciated in the silence of being. Clarity and peace would permeate the stillness.

No conflict would be present as the mind would be free from its cycle of dissatisfaction-desire-temporary satisfaction. The organism would experience fullness in the moment of stillness. To move our little finger, to swallow, to adjust our back in this stillness would be to disturb ten thousand universes. In stillness neither questions nor answers matter. A sharp, unmoving abiding embraces the faint vibration of a body poised on the edge of time.

Cross legged, sitting on a chair or stool, the meditator sits with erect back and closed eyes in a state of alertness. He or she enters an absorbed repose, to experience rest, a state of equilibrium, a depth of meditation. Accessibility to this realm becomes available, worthwhile attaining since it means our relentless mental excursions will not have the tormenting grip of constant agitation. Realizing that a disorderly life constructs a disorderly mind, we turn to meditation to uncover the silent depths of being and to cut through the restlessness.

Stillness transforms the psyche. A different order of knowledge flowers from sublime stillness, born of receptive attention and non-reactivity. This special knowing ends the cycles of painful unrest. There is a depth of peace that defies circumstances. All transitory events of the immediate world come to rest. Exhausting reactivity, consciousness discovers contentment, a refuge from swinging between different mental states.

However, stillness does not materialize with a snap of the fingers. Lack of familiarity places stillness in the unknown. The new meditator can only imagine the experience of deep contentment. The known is mental movement in many forms, pleasant and unpleasant. Those who follow the way of serious and sustained meditation embark on an adventurous field. A useful way to discover the value of deep meditation is through participating in a retreat. Initially the meditator may face waves of turbulence and tiredness before descending into calmness and being at ease with existence. We must remember that life is organic not mechanistic stasis.

A human being consists of the interdependence of body, feelings, perceptions, thoughts and consciousness. These parts make up a whole. The interaction of these parts affects the whole. Awareness of the whole affects the parts. Sitting still in meditation with straight back, mindfully allows the interacting parts to settle. In that stillness and harmony inwardly and outwardly, there is a sense of Totality, where others, the environment and ourselves matter equally since they are inseparable.

But the organic nature of the mind means the meditator cannot presume that sitting mindfully without movement will guarantee the discovery of stillness and Totality. From a mechanistic viewpoint the meditation instructions are supposed to lead to a desired end, but sitting still does not assure inner stillness. It is, instead, the fruit of an undemanding moment-to-moment mindfulness. Techniques of meditation can neither produce nor engineer such spiritual depths of being. Precise instructions give some support to the quality of relaxed attention, but techniques play a minor function in reaching spiritual depths.

So what happens? The agitated mind that brought a person to meditate in the first place is only magnified. What was never intended to happen is happening. Like homeopathic doctors, who say "Things may get worse before they get better," the meditation teacher is obliged to reassure the meditation students that "It's normal, everybody goes through this stage." Streams of thoughts come and go in relentlessly. Genuine contentment with the organic and changing nature of the mind seems elusive. Meditation thus reveals the lack of a substantial or controlling self and the imperfection of idealism. Preoccupation with self constantly flashes into the field of attention during meditation.

All these preoccupations are an indirect form of advice to surrender notions of achieving perfection. We may need to understand and accommodate our personality before depths are touched. The transforming power of stillness dissolves preoccupation with self. In meditation, clinging and attachment to the activities of self-interest wither away because the nature of mind becomes transparent. In this way inner peace contributes to peace in the world. Often the mind imagines the task of inner transformation is beyond reach—even before exploration has begun. Those who resist meditation may think that Totality and the flowering of a gracious and liberating awareness are not accessible, even that it is going against human nature to seek them.

While fermenting over states of mind, there is an avoidance of facing existence through stillness and silence. To ignore meditation, and the potential for release of insights in meditation, is a major error of the spiritual life. Dismissing meditation is to pass by a profound sense of presence. When we reject such quietude, we neglect the grace of an awesome subliminal magnitude that knows no boundary. Sitting still in a silent meditative mindfulness, alone or in the company of others, is a time-honoured spiritual tradition for enlightenment. Realizations emerge through direct experience rather than grasping upon what is read.

Stillness manifests free from the duality of striving for one thing and reacting against something else. Touched by stillness we discover that everything naturally falls into place. Breath flows in and out, a thought appears and vanishes in consciousness, light trickles under the closed eyelids, distant sounds grace the ear, warm sensations dance gently in the body's cellular life. The obvious expressions of movement from the surrounding world do not obscure stillness. Stillness naturally deepens through experiencing the absence of reactivity.

Stillness captures an unspoken mystery, a transcendent song communicating through our deepest recesses. Even ego, conditioned by our reactions, loses meaning. The appearance of self is seen as expressing the unknown rather than obscuring it. It is as though we have come full circle. At first we believed that we had to know ourselves through looking into our personal reactivity to situations and ourselves. But ultimately life does not work like that. Immensity and "good" and "bad" forms of reaction belong to the nature of things, not just to stillness.

In lying horizontal facing up to the night sky,
In sitting still on a deserted beach,
In the gentle paddle of a boat on a windless lake,
The appetite for this and that is over.
In that utterly becalmed state of being
the call of the owl reverberates
across the universe.
In the stillness of the night,
Walls evaporate into nothingness.
In motionless standing on the hilltop
God fills the air.

The body breathes into the sublime nature of things, reactivity belongs not to ourselves, but to what is unfathomable, beyond human comprehension. We realize that the Mystery of things is revealed equally in the pits of reactivity, in the orgy of evil, and in sublime stillness. We are left profoundly humbled. God is revealed equally in Heaven and Hell.

Part Five
The Immeasurable

CHAPTER TWENTY-ONE

ENLIGHTENMENT, NEAR OR FAR

In the religious texts of the East the account of the Buddha's enlightenment set the tone for generations of spiritual practitioners. The focus for the spiritual life became a quest, a relentless search for realization that would overshadow all other experiences. Enlightenment mattered, enlightenment counted.

The unenlightened engaged in the pursuit of enlightenment: the release from suffering and a superficial life. The words of the Buddha would ring in the minds of the seekers who flew towards another plane of existence.

"I searched for the unsurpassed state of security that is Nirvana. I did attain this utter peace. Spiritual wisdom and insight arose in me. Sure is my release.... This Truth (Dharma) is profound, hard to see, hard to understand, excellent, pre-eminent, beyond the sphere of thinking, subtle and to be penetrated by the wise alone."

"Open is the door to the Deathless for those who listen and have renounced clinging to beliefs."

People fashioned their lives to suit the quest—as wanderers, monks, nuns, householders and as students of spiritual teachers. They experienced the disciplines of ethics, devotion, inquiry, meditation and service. They listened earnestly to spiritual teachings. The opportunity for enlightenment was available in the activity of listening to transmission of teachings on spiritual realization. Every skilful spiritual practice imaginable could be employed to cherish and sustain the pursuit of the summum bonum of existence.

In practical terms, we today can listen to teachings and explore a method of spiritual training that embraces a three fold concern, namely morality, meditative awareness and wisdom. A life committed to the morality of nonharming in personal, financial and social life is the foundation for enlightened existence. This morality refuses to support to those who abuse life, no matter what the rationale. Living a moral and mindful life leaves little opportunity for submission to consumer interests. Morality is a way of being in the world not a means for proclaiming self righteousness. A moral life includes the total character and conduct of the individual or society. Otherwise all are debased. Violence and corruption destroy the very fabric of human relationships. Pernicious, self-seeking behaviour denies morality.

We live in an era of rampant egotism, contaminated by self-serving beliefs and organizations. Ego, desire and conflict are the normal behaviour among our public figures and in our institutions. There is no ongoing public debate on values and morality in our society. Genuine concerns for social and environmental harmony are neglected in the ruthless competition of the profit-making culture. Ethics, integrity and compassion are not on the agenda. When morality is confused with self righteousness then sanctimonious attitudes prevail. The world becomes divided between the righteous and the guilty; a form of morality born from the ego's wish to affirm itself. Morality is an expression of genuine goodness not a basis for condemning others.

Morality serves as a foundation for awareness and meditative insights. The opportunity for meditation and quiet reflection supports the development of a human being. Meditation touches depths within inaccessible to thought, to the movement of desire. In stillness we are receptive to the Here and Now. Deep qualities of heart and mind touch consciousness. This meditative awareness enables a human being to flower. There is no need to identify in meditation with a particular methodology. Meditation methods and techniques are secondary to stillness and silence. Without the experience of silence and stillness, it becomes easy to get bogged down in the demands of self, issues and society. Insight meditation dissolves notions of the mind as the centre of the world, exposing the emptiness of "I" and "my." In stillness the measuring of circumstances has no purpose. From silence of being comes clear action and a sublime and resolute kindness for all. Meditation is not confined to a posture or timetable but is the outcome of realizing the significance of the Here and Now.

Morality-meditation-wisdom support each other. The maturing of this threefold process ends conflicts and the confusing array of choices. The whole being is alert and sensitive to the moment, to the daily life issues embraced in this three fold awareness. In meditation there is an innocence that renders notions of time and religious promises irrelevant. To witness what is present with an effortless commitment enables integration into daily life. Morality reveals the light of wisdom, wisdom reveals morality. Meditation communicates directly what is beyond conventional considerations, and simultaneously influences our presence in the world. The fulfilment of morality, meditation and wisdom rests in the Ultimate Truth.

Along with inspirations from religious texts are personal accounts of religious experiences. The enlightened proclaim the sanctity and imminence of transcendence, that enlightenment is no joke. Serious meditation and insightful experiences eradicates ignorance, conceit and self-cherishing. It also provides the opportunity to discover spiritual depths. There is the capacity for people to explore together their values and experiences and to share their wisdom. The threefold values of morality, meditation and wisdom express an integrity that generates an enlightened life and compassionate action.

Enlightenment can seem far removed from ritualistic daily behaviour. There is comfort in the knowledge that ordinary existence can be transformed. But such a goal must be pursued with humility. The seeker of Truth may feel unease hearing yet another witness of transcendence. "God came into my life and saved me and He can do the same for you" is the attitude of those who make a fuss about their experiences. Descriptions of spiritual experiences change; they can become exaggerated. Life-changing experiences may give the mind a sense of arrival, which ends the spiritual search. But at subtle levels, conceit can still undermine any profound spiritual experience. There are those who wisely make no claims to enlightenment. Realization of such a state shows itself in morality, meditation and ultimate wisdom.

Excessive reference to enlightenment grants it a metaphysical status. It enters into the realms of the distant and unattainable. Through constant repetition, the gap between That and the ordinary grows. Once the gulf is present it has to be bridged. The seeker becomes a prisoner to means and end. Hypnotized by spiritual concepts, confusion ensues. Obsession with means become instrumental in determining the countless spiritual models that give rise to differences and conflict.

Spellbound by language, mesmerized by words, infatuated with concepts, interpretations of Truth take form. Adherents are thus born. Those who proclaim allegiance to particular teachings are afraid of doubts. Exalting certain words, religious statues, altars, sacred books or a photograph of a guru reduces Ultimate Truth to personal impressions. The religious paraphernalia becomes special, alleged to represent "something." It is a travesty of spiritual life to reduce enlightened wisdom to the assembly of items on an altar. The Profound transcends memorabilia.

Certain teachings encourage the preservation of impressions and objects instead of spiritual inquiry. Truth is forgotten. Blindness or ignorance reaches such lengths that the Truth is mixed up in experiences of bliss, clinging and concepts. What is profound is overlooked in the doctrine of words and in the mists of feelings. Purity, goodness, saintliness, martyrdom, religious experiences become attainable objects, fascinations for the mind. Clinging to experiences and attainments hinders full spiritual awakening.

Those radicals who rebel against spiritual authority show confidence in their own authority. Wisdom and compassion take priority over the location of an authority. Yet often various spiritual powers squash this spontaneous movement towards liberation and an enlightened way of being. Those seekers who rebel are often dismissed for refusing to conform to the present line of authority. This leaves only the conformists lost in their pride and self-delusion. Those who think of themselves as on the outside fare no better; embittered, judgmental and hostile they perpetuate divisiveness. Negativity and resentment hinder any serious attempt to analyse the virtues and failings of any spiritual practice. Yet an element of creativity, sophistication, warmth and expansiveness persists in some people. The heart and mind are willing to acknowledge the spiritual undertakings of others, willing to give a fair assessment of respective paths through inquiry and mutual exploration. This tolerant and supportive vein is the saving grace.

Wisdom points to That beyond the involved mind. It could be considered a significant breakthrough in perception to question whether or not anything lies beyond the involved mind. Right in the midst of commitment we might wonder what is outside of this preoccupation. The human being has spotted a hole in the wall. Looking through the hole to what is beyond reveals Totality.

The step by step systematic approach supports a mechanistic view of spiritual life. First you do this. Then you do that. After you have completed that, you go on to this, and finally enlightenment—after weeks, years or lifetimes. It sounds reasonable. The spiritual authority comes across as sure of himself or herself and the follower wants to be able to describe experiences in the same way. The stronger the impressions and convictions about the descriptions, the stronger the clinging to beliefs. Enlightenment, which is the cessation of suffering, is neglected on the way to becoming clones.

Some teachers proclaim there is no way. There is absolutely nothing you can do, no practice you can develop, no path you can walk. This may be interpreted as useful since it guards against burial in mechanistic approaches to the fulfilment of spiritual awakening. But believing nothing can be done to gain enlightenment brings other consequences. To go so far and find out there is nothing one can do is a shock to the system. To turn around and go back to abject existence is another. Rather than scuttle back into drudgery, the seeker is likely to become a follower, repeating the "there is nothing you can do" line. Such a believer waits to be among the chosen who are spontaneously enlightened.

At its best, the no-way school throws a person back to nowhere and he or she may be galvanized into a shock, an awakening, that doesn't include any form of hero worship or repetitive spiritual practice. But that's improbable. The no-way school is likely to produce another unfortunate self-deception. This school tends to be patronizing, ridiculing the followers of spiritual exploration. Dissatisfied practitioners of any spiritual path are vulnerable to joining the ranks of "everything is already perfect" schools of spirituality. Those who believe in the way to enlightenment and those who believe in no-way offer little spiritual comfort. Both kinds of believers get stuck when they champion one side of this dualism or the other. The Emptiness of spiritual absolutism is liberating and enlightening.

Realization reveals nothing is what it seems to be. Emptiness makes all views possible, yet there is the emptiness of Emptiness. There is nobody to recommend, nobody to persuade to join the ranks. Nothing whatsoever is worth being identified with. To abide with an enlightened wisdom is freedom from all forms of spiritual attachment and identification. There is a sublime joy and inexhaustible love that pervades. The heart cannot restrict itself to a set of beliefs.

If we are not sure whether or not we are identified with a way or with no-way, then it maybe wise to ask for the frank view of others. If the response is "Yes, I think you are identified with ..." that could show the seeds of conflict are present amidst the self-satisfaction of the identification. The feeling of being right and that others are wrong reinforces the dualistic perceptions. Self seeks its advantage point. Emptiness reveals the limitation of wielding a position as a weapon. Those who have discovered a liberating and enlightening way of being refuse to perpetuate the forces of ignorance and conflict. The world may fight them but they do not fight the world.

Those who never enter the dynamic of descriptions may be afraid to open their mouths.

Those who never enter into the dynamic of descriptions might be expressing wisdom.

Those who express a position may be showing wisdom.

Those who don't take up a position may be showing wisdom.

Those who take up the position of having no position may be incurable!

Those who express the position of having no position may be wise.

CHAPTER TWENTY-TWO

COMMITMENT TO THE TRUTH

To be serious in the quest for Truth is to live with integrity. It is taking risks in the passion for Truth. If we identify only with the idea of Truth we remain secure with the old and familiar, forsaking the immediacy of Truth for our notions about it. It means we have given up infinite discovery and settled for an inferior version to which we then subordinate our existence. Living the Truth is never a simple undertaking. It requires cutting through our conditioned convictions to realize the nature of things.

In the conventional world, Truth often becomes expendable, used to uphold a viewpoint, or modified to fit circumstances. Some people speak what they consider the Truth regardless of the effects, while others have no regard for the Truth. When we communicate what we think is truthful, we state what we perceive. We may have very strong feelings around a particular perception, but wish to avoid expressing them; or we may express strong feelings around an issue when we are not really concerned. The listener may accept what he or she hears as Truth, or experience doubts, or openly condemn every statement as false.

Truth is useful and pragmatic when it contributes to our understanding. It establishes trust, and has the potential to change our lives. We continually try to find reasons why events take place. Hearing painful news, we are likely to leap straight away into the "why?" questioning mode. We want to get to the Truth of things. But we soon lose interest: there is often a lack of passion to realize the Ultimate Truth. Getting to the conventional truth of things is finding the cause or causes. Cause and effect is conventionally true; spiritual awakening is finding the Ultimate Truth, not tied to cause and effect.

In everyday exploration of Truth, communication with others is obviously important, including reflecting back the points that others are making. Instead of presuming to understand the message, we repeat the gist of what we heard to see whether or not it is accurate. We often naively believe that we know what someone means without checking with them first. Preconceptions about what others mean when they speak are the curse of Truth.

Skill in reflecting messages pays respect to the communication of others, and shows assumptions do not paralyse us. Mirroring precisely another's words enables the descriptive mode to become a tool for comprehension. We are less likely to be harsh and reactive or mindlessly take on board the views of others. Listening attentively, asking for further information and reflecting it back allows others the opportunity to clarify for themselves their views or involvement in a situation. Both parties are then able to remain in tune with each other, to follow each other's line of thought and reach a mutual understanding of an issue—even if they beg to differ.

In practical terms this means paying attention to six aspects of communication:

Awareness of the event, related circumstances and behaviour. Realizing the interdependent nature of various conditions and views is necessary in order to relate what happened, is happening or will happen.

Feelings follow from the event and to it; these feelings are pleasant or painful or somewhere in between.

Thoughts occur about the event which influence and give shape to the issue.

Motivation influences the type of communication, whether through language or action.

States of mind arising in communication can stimulate further desires, projections and fantasies.

Lack of inherent existence is a feature of all communications. The issue is the known. There are multiple unknown factors.

Communication intimates the unknown as much as the known. The unknown embraces as much as the known, and is inseparable from it. Thoughts isolate an event from other events. If we take a viewpoint and give it special existence we isolate it from everything else. Isolation is treated as Ultimate Truth rather than conventional. By recognizing its relative value we allow the construction of the standpoint to fall into the vast scheme of things.

Staying with the perceived truth when we describe things paves the way for insights into the situation. Rather than proclaim, we interpret: "I believe that..." "I think that..." "I experience that...." When we forget the value of this way of communicating we make claims on the Truth. "The Truth is..." "Everybody is..." or "Nobody wants to...." When we make claims on the Truth or generalize people's experience we become ensnared in "for" or "against" judgements. Our interpretation becomes a view, which we have to promote and defend. Absorbed into our thoughts, feelings and reactions, we become trapped in certainties such as: "always," "every time," or "never."

Awareness of lack of inherent existence reveals that we can never have all the information. Presence supports absence, absence supports presence. One cannot be without the other. Skill in listening and asking for further information to clarify the known helps process the information and makes way for understanding. Concentration contributes towards understanding the relationship of ourselves to others. If we imagine that our truths or ourselves have inherent existence we fall into generalities. "Life is difficult" or "the world is in a terrible mess." These generalities may sound inconsequential, but such a viewpoint may indicate a range of feelings, thoughts and motivations affecting our personality and behaviour. Communication skills include shifting from the general to the specific. Such communication deals with clear examples rather than vague, generalized ideas. General views obscure wisdom. The Ultimate Truth embraces both the general and the specific.

This means that instead of holding forth a view as solid and absolute we change our language into a description of relationship to events. We free ourselves from a fixation on an apparent object such as ourselves, truth or life. This contributes enormously to our understanding of the nature of interdependent circumstances. Another way we employ universals is by speaking in "you" or "we" language conveying the idea that everybody experiences events in the same way as "I." It is often better to let go of universal conclusions about people, and keep specifically to "I" as the framework of both interpretative and descriptive language.

To report factually our experience allows for a precision not available when we speak in general terms.

We imagine cause and effect thinking as Ultimate Truth. "This is the effect of that." This caused that to happen." "This effect is now becoming the cause for something else." Cause and effect thinking explains the reasons for "events." It can however stop us from deep inquiry. We ask "why?" and produce an answer which satisfies us and then we go back to sleep. Cause and effect thinking can trigger different reasons that stop us from sleeping! We are constantly explaining away what makes something happen. Having worked out the reasons, we then reasonably suppose that the same events will occur again if the same causes are present. But we also produce waves of uncertainty about what we think the Truth is.

We explore events by discovering what contributes to suffering and what does not. We may have to consider what changes we are willing to make. Various diverse, sequential and interdependent circumstances contribute to the way things appear. For clarity, peace of mind and appropriate action it becomes necessary to reflect on the way conditions influence the rise and fall of events. This may include learning to ask questions at the right time in the right place. The conditions for the questions are as relevant as the conditions for the answers. This is not an intellectual exercise; it is an exploration of heartfelt interest to realize the Truth. We often assume knowledge of cause and effect without commitment to investigating the processes. With superficial information of causal factors we draw quick conclusions. Hasty decisions follow on. And we make decisions with the desire to have a quick effect. Such analysis of a situation in the world of conventional truths leads to reactive behaviour.

Constantly thinking about an issue contaminates and corrupts it. When we become involved, we continue to imagine that our thoughts are an independent statement about the event. We forget thoughts make the event! Fixed conclusions give the impression the subject matter had some inherent self-existence removed from the rest of the process.

Subjective interpretation and objective facts are something of a smoke screen in the world of conventional truths. Each truth tries to affirm itself over another. By not clinging to assumptions we can understand the process of events while responding wholeheartedly to them. Views expressed with balance and integrity represent the conventional world that thoughtful mortals appreciate. Ultimately we can establish nothing in its own right. When we make this clear we pay respect to the Truth. Wisdom is knowing the difference between description and projections.

We tend to attribute Ultimate Truth to conventional statements, but what we say either makes great, little or no difference. When we cling to inherent existence we hold onto views of permanence or impermanence. If we disregard conventional truth, we hold onto a nihilistic view. This denies the influence of skilful and unskilful actions, personal responsibility, and cause and effect. Emptiness allows us to see the foolishness of abiding in either views of permanence, impermanence or nihilism.

Conviction can also lead to an absolutist position—"the only way." Absolutism pays no respect to conventional or Ultimate Truth. A person simply feels very strongly about his or her view of an issue. Absolutists impose their views on others insisting tenaciously on their truth. No amount of communication skills can untangle a deeply entrenched view when the individual is adamantly self-righteous. "My mind is made up. Whatever takes place in this communication won't make any difference." Unexamined thoughts, feeling and motivations support intransigence. One way to avoid drawing fixed conclusions is remembering to communicate in a non-absolutist way; after all, language only reflects a set of views.

Clear communication is mindful of the dangers of absolutism; it states the current perception from experience and allows for change. Quality communication does not occur merely by introducing the occasional qualifying statement into our language. Commitment to the Truth is revealed through contact with events as they occur and change *at the time*. This expresses moment-to-moment wisdom, giving the opportunity to respond in fresh and dynamic ways. We respond with wisdom to events. By neither solidifying an issue nor denying its presence, there is scope for liberating insights.

"Good" or "bad" judgements mirror the vested interests of an individual or group. We then believe that good and bad exist in the event itself rather than understanding the judgmental mind at work. Those who believe they know what is good for us have often generated harm. Conflict and pain occur in identification with cause and effect, the character of relative truth. We use language to solidify situations into something static. Nouns name a person, place, thing, quality or action. Through the habitual use of nouns to name and adjectives to describe, we form hard views that make up our conception of the conventional world. We imagine we are referring exclusively to reality, but we are also referring to our mental constructions.

Mindfulness of speech contributes to wisdom and compassion. We are challenged to communicate wisely and directly despite hostility. We may have to breathe our way through vindictive statements and condemnation of our beliefs and actions. Silence is sometimes the wise response. The bedfellow of absolutism is extremism and a disregard for wisdom. Emptiness of independent existence of the spoken or written word is the revealed Truth.

Relative truth is referred to dogmatically, it gains a "thingness." Relative truths belong to the world of description. No position is final, nothing can arise in its own right and so nothing can pass alone. Absolutism and cause and effect belong to a human interpretation. It is not even necessary to try to negate the appearance of relative truth to establish Ultimate Truth. That would only give relative truth an inherent existence.

Language does not affect Ultimate Truth. Ultimate Truth does not rely on language, social conventions, rights and wrongs and the range of ordinary truths and falsehoods that humanity communicates. Ultimate Truth is realizing the lack of inherent existence of whatever we turn our attention to. It is neither metaphysical nor abstract. This Truth is empty of substance, realizable and equally present in all circumstances. The significance of Ultimate Truth is that it sets us free. It is the Truth which liberates; neither our own efforts nor the efforts of another can do that.

Furthermore, Ultimate Truth absorbs the conventional truths of life. Realization of Truth frees us from pain and the unsatisfactory conventions of selfish desires and fears. Nothing can be said to change or remain the same owing to lack of inherent existence. The Vastness of the process is such that it knows neither beginning nor ending, nor coming or going. This is spoken of as Ultimate since nothing lies outside its scope.

Spiritual concepts are prone to being thought of as Ultimate Truth. There is a danger that separating conventional truths from

Ultimate Truth makes the Ultimate into a inherent object. The wisdom of Emptiness gives the space to understand what is called relative truth and what is Ultimate. This understanding responds to people and events without being bound to them or their actions. Spiritual enlightenment is as available as colour to a person with sound eyesight. Since there is neither affirmation nor negation of conventional truth, there is nothing to gain or get rid of. Ultimate Truth reveals a Freedom from being bound to any expression of Truth. There is nothing certain about cause and effect, impermanence, permanence, birth and death, arrival and departure. The enlightened ones see the unsatisfactoriness of identifying with conventional truths and effortlessly respond to others' suffering caused through such blindness.

CHAPTER TWENTY-THREE

WHO AM I?

Beliefs often seem to act like an empty shadow obscuring Truth. People committed to Western religious beliefs and people committed to Western scientific beliefs engage in an uncomfortable struggle for supremacy. The question of the origins of the world and the destiny of life arouse intense passions, and opposing views appear narrow, heretical or dangerous. Those of other persuasion are blamed for identifying with their views and lacking understanding of other views.

The religious believer and the scientist reveal a genuine sincerity for their cherished views of the world. Each holds the opinion that only one of them has the legitimate perspective on the origin of life and that the other is wrong. As a result, religion and science continue to quarrel over the distant past, as if the origin of the species had some special relationship to Truth.

Western religious believers have launched one campaign after another to convert us to their theories about our origins and destiny. The dogma that "we are all born sinners" has harmed personal, social and environmental life. The emotional impact of such beliefs includes guilt, insecurity and lack of self worth. A piece of graffiti written on the wall of a London church said: "God hasn't forgotten the world but He's now working on less ambitious projects." Scientists have equally foisted their beliefs upon us, claiming that matter composed of subatomic particles is the basis of existence. Their belief in the breakdown of matter and sophisticated technology has its intellectual consequences, including the desire to control and manipulate the environment with little regard for ethics. Debates between religion and science are often intellectual games with scientific research and religious texts being major distractions to genuine enquiry, deeper values and a holistic vision.

Scientists, armed with microscopes and mathematical formulae, conclude with impressive sophistication that life is energy—with various forces forming organic matter changing and evolving in time and space. Scientists love elaborate conceptual models of the nature of existence. Each fresh theory, hypothesis or elaboration of old theory brings them stature. His or her standing in the scientific community matters as much as the theory to the scientist. Getting to the Truth of things often becomes a smoke screen for the elevation of self. The perception of the observer or experiencer of events is integral to findings and conclusions, a fact which modern science is beginning to discover. Often religious believers and scientists imagine they can stand outside of life, whilst loving to make pronouncements about the way it began and the way it will end.

It is easy to ridicule cherished religious and scientific beliefs. No matter how bizarre these beliefs nor how reasonable the views of origin and destiny, ultimate proof is not available. So the religionist and the scientist, the creationist and the evolutionist, unite in their adversity towards each other's beliefs. Can we examine our existence beginning from an ordinary and simple proposition?

I find myself as a particular person in this world. In the past I experienced birth and at some future date I will experience death. Before birth I do not know whether I was or whether I was not. After death I do not know whether I will exist or not. Does before birth or after death have any significance outside of my beliefs? My life is a field of experience. I participate in a process of events. I see that the world, as I perceive it, affects and changes me. As an entity in this vast field of life, I influence, affect and change the world in gross and subtle ways. I experience attraction and aversion to situations and experiences. I get caught up in my ideas about the world and end up wondering why I praise and condemn events as though this was the Truth. I think that I can separate the world from my perception of it. I think I know the difference between being objective and subjective but experience doubts.

Am I anything more than a collection of ideas generated through thought, words and action? Is this idea of "me" nothing more than that? Is "me" perhaps another unprovable idea—as far flung as the significance of Adam and Eve biting the apple or the

ape straightening its back? Awareness reveals mortality, our existence propped up between birth and death. We look at the world's
population; they share the same predicament—one entity dwelling amidst other entities between birth and death. In this perceived phenomena I feel desperate to find out if this is what it all
boils down to—entities experiencing birth, ageing, pain and
death, and the proliferation of countless ideas, perceptions and
feelings.

I turn my mind's eye back to my childhood. I laughed and
cried. I was naughty and playful. I was a child and I became an
adult. Throughout these experiences, from the wailing, gurgling
baby to the imaginative, stroppy child to the blooming and
immature adolescent, "I" am the same person. The feeling of
"me", the notion of "I" hasn't really altered at all. I was like that. I
am like this. I will be like that. All these experiences happened to
me, who remained the same throughout the years. Pleasure, pain
or equanimity do not disturb the essential "me." The fluctuating
mental and emotional life does not intrude upon "me." If that is
the truth, it renders meaningless all efforts to change myself since
"I" cannot be changed. Jettisoning some of the unpleasant experiences is welcome, but "I" feel permanently established as long as
I live.

I reflect further about myself. My body is very different from
that of my childhood years. Many people would not recognize
who I am today if they saw a photograph of me as a child.
Despite the generally similar configuration—head on shoulders,
trunk on legs—nothing much else appears similar. These physical
changes apply mentally as well. My feelings and thoughts are
very different today compared to those of my childhood. At least,
most of the time! I do not think, speak or act as a baby. On the one
side, I claim I am precisely the same person through the years. If
so, I am constant, immutable and can never progress or regress.
On the other side I claim that I am very different from what I was
years ago.

Am I different from who I used to be? If so, it is a different person writing this page from the one who began the first page. If I
have changed in the flow of time how can I accept any responsibility for what I did in the past? Yet I bear the fruits of past
actions, willingly or not. It seems that when I refer to "me"
remaining the same throughout life I am referring only to the con-

cept and nothing else. Then it seems as if "I" am just a concept. That seems strange, cold and detached.

I cannot with certainty say I am an unchanging self since it denies my experience. Yet, equally, I cannot say I am a changing self since it also denies my experience. I cannot proclaim that I am just an idea nor otherwise. Well, who am I? What am I?" I wonder. I meditate. I reflect. I read books on philosophy, religion, mysticism, science. Who is reading the books? Who is reading this page? I can't conclude there is an unchanging self, a changing one, both or neither. I continue to wrestle with the issue perhaps wanting to conclude that I consist of both, one part changing, one part unchanging. I can't separate and hold onto one part from the other. By definition a changing part can't affect an unchanging part. If it did it would not be an unchanging part. A changing part cannot be separated from an unchanging part.

My view of myself and others becomes increasingly more awkward. In the effort to find a resolution to the issue of self I posit yet another viewpoint. "I have no self." Information from certain Buddhist traditions, as well as from scientists, supports this view. Self is denying self. I experience no real evidence to confirm a consistent self and no real evidence to deny it—outside ways of thinking about myself. Am I, or am I not? If I am, what am I? If I am not (what I think I am) then what am I? I think therefore I am what? I think therefore I am not?

As inquiry continues and deepens I begin to feel a certain ease within—having passed through waves of dis-ease. My deeper intimations reveal that I carry packaged opinions. I use them ad nauseam to describe myself. I think some of them matter more than others. Yet every opinion of who I am is only an opinion. Outside of opinion I cannot be said to have an existence or a non-existence. I begin to feel rather grounded in these revelations. I have not turned up an answer to who I am, but I am no longer persecuted by the question.

The inquiry shifts away from the expertise of those who try to define who I am. They might describe me through my cells, my roles, my appearances, my thought processes, attitudes, or achievements. What they see is not what I am. What I see is not who I am either. Yet I cannot honestly form a view that I am something other. I investigate deeply into "who am I?". I begin to see that I employ the concept "I" or "me" or "myself" to refer to this mind-body process. I move past the stage of blanket affirmation or blanket denial of self. Both are only the product of thought.

I say "I am well." "I am young." "I am thin." I may say that the body is the object or content of my attention. But the "I" as a deeply rooted notion appears almost simultaneously, so there is almost immediate identification with the body. "I am sitting here." Is it "I" sitting here or is it the body sitting here? Since the body is the object how can it be "I" since "I" is the subject? If "I" is the object then is there another "I" that is the subject? Is there one "I", two "I"s or multiple "I"s? It starts to get confusing again. My relationship to this body changes. Instead of total identification with my body—"I am breathing in and I am breathing out" —I view this body as a possession—"my breath," "my back", "my headache." This relationship to body implies a "me" separate from body.

The "I" also arises in a similar relationship to the world of sense objects over which I make claims. My book (what is seen) my tape cassette (what is heard), my flowers (what is smelt), my food (what is tasted), my armchair (what is touched). These sensations become possessions. Personal claims over momentary events through repeated use of "my" torment the mind. At such times, we forget that "my" is a charged concept. "My country, right or wrong," for example shows how dangerous such thinking can be. I am mindful of identification with anything, such as beginning a sentence with "I am...." I also notice when I am possessive about an event and when I am not.

The company chairman owned a house in an expensive mews in the centre of the city. He was working in the office when he received a telephone call from a friend who lived a street away from his home. "I have some terrible news to report to you. There is smoke coming out of your roof. Your house is on fire." The man panicked. "My house, my home, my antiques, my paintings, my books!" Stricken with terror, he raced out to the lift and shot down to the reception to run to the car park. Just as he passed the desk on the ground floor a receptionist shouted: "There's a phone call for you, sir. It's very urgent." The frantic man lurched over, grabbed the phone and said with great impatience, "Yes, quickly." It was his friend again. "I'm terribly sorry. I made an awful mistake. It was not your house. It was next door that was on fire." The chairman said: "Not my house. What a relief."

The businessman's suffering and anguish related to his house and his possessions. Attachment to possessions obscures the true wealth of life. Wearily, the man returned to his desk. The phone rang yet again. It was his friend. "Look, I hate to have to tell you this but the flames have spread to the roof of your place." "To my roof" he cried in desperation again. "Where the hell is the fire brigade!?" What we possess and claim as "mine" we care about more than anything else in the world. We do not bother much about what is not mine.

The more grasping, the stronger the "my;"
The greater the "my" the more suffering of self,
The more suffering of self,
The greater the loss of wisdom and compassion,
This is the everyday pattern of things.

Reification of the object, the imposition of specialness, reinforces the "me" who owns or knows the object. The status given to the object, be it physical, emotional or ideas, intensifies a range of projections particularly the tendency to relate to objects as mine. But lurking in the background is the shadow of loss and change. Identification with the body means "I" draw fixed conclusions—of being finite, limited, ageing and doomed to death. By exploring the conditioned arising and passing of "I" and "my," we can have liberating insights which alter this view. All experiential phenomena are contents of consciousness. Emotions, moods, thoughts, preferences connect to "I" and "my." Thinking and talking about "me" and "my" can become imprisoning unless we understand the relativity of "I" and "my." To the question "who am I?" I might understandably conclude: "I am whatever I am identified with in that moment." I might despair and draw the conclusion "Oh no, this is how I am." I might act on that conclusion. "I have to do something about it. I can't go on living in this prison of identification with content and experience"

There are times when any substantial "I" or "my" is lacking; in deep sleep, deep meditation, the sense of oneness and unselfish love. When these moments pass, sweet and divine as they may be, the old pattern resurfaces. "This happened to me. It didn't happen to anybody else!" Yet again, "I" asserts itself as that in which experiences are validated. In stillness, silence and insight, the propensity towards identification and grasping onto mental-physical states fades into obscurity. Awareness becomes a clear presence embracing the world of mind, body and environment. "I" is slow to arise, and separate phenomena are slow to stand out. But then "I" may identify itself with awareness as an Unchanging Self in which the changing mental-physical life appears.

Is this who I am? Is this the consummation of the inquiry? "I" and "my" loses its grip around mind-body-objects but grasps awareness instead. Objects, mind and body are no longer seen to belong to self. Then identification takes place with pure awareness, pure and luminous. Awareness is not worth grasping either, though it is the subject for objects. The claim that awareness is inherent and beyond content is unprovable.

Awareness is not the centre of Immensity. I am not at the centre of Immensity. There is no centre to Immensity. I realize that I cannot define who I am. I realize that I cannot lay claim to any ultimate expression of myself. Since the Ultimate Truth of all things is Inexpressible then birth, change and death, subject and object are conventional notions. These notions are bound to the belief in a substantial "I". Enlightenment exposes the emptiness of "I."

Nothing to take up,
Nothing to be possessive about,
Recognizing "I" and "my" as conventions,
Freedom shines,
When acting without "self" delusion,
Peace reigns in all that is called subject-object.

CHAPTER TWENTY-FOUR

THE FIRE FOR CHANGE

There is such a complexity to our daily life that it seems to conspire to stop us from knowing the depths of ourselves and our existence. Our attention grabs self and other, subject and object. We live our life from day to day with little meaningful interruption. Our daily concerns around mechanical and social events consume our existence. Revelations of exquisite phenomenal existence are far from our lives, which remain painfully ordinary. This familiar trek through known territory extinguishes the bright flame of vision. Our wretched conformity to social and peer expectations smothers us. Sometimes we experience claustrophobia, a suffocating restriction of circumstances that seems impossible to overcome. But like a chicken in its shell, this imprisonment provides security. Within our gloomy shell-like existence we live out an unconscious indifference to the miracle of life. In our boredom and helplessness, we muddle through the day unable to break free from the drabness of this mundane security.

We sometimes embellish this numbing conformity with the naive fantasy that others live a greater life. We envy the megastars of entertainment, politics and sport. The leading figures in soap operas, the rich, the beautiful and the handsome recount their "success" stories, omitting admission of dependency on alcohol and sleeping tablets to cope with anxiety and depression. The life of the stars only seems full of excitement because our life appears small and inconsequential in comparison. Our internalized inner resentment and self hatred only encourage idealized projections onto others as compensation for the unconscious shame of what we have made of our life and what society has made of us. We view our daily experiences as a succession of mini-activities, an endless trail of jobs that have to be done.

· However, this treadmill can spur a revolt against the endless routine. Some people living in such a vanquished state find rebellion in the depth of their being. They become determined to listen earnestly to their inner yearnings, to feel the fire for change, for something greater. Anger, frustration and envy arise as warped protests against this way of being. But we subordinate our lives to our ambitions, or resignations, by habitually identifying ourselves with the daily commuter, or forty hour per week employee. We are pale, grey, impoverished figures; our playfulness, innocence and capacity to celebrate life are sacrificed on the altar of conventional existence.

Confinement to the kitchen sink and the commuter train become symbols of spiritual poverty when we know that we hate this way of life. Where is the fire for deep spiritual experiences when the hands are buried in soapy dishwater? Where is the enlightened vision when waiting for the train to work on a rain-swept morning? Why is the flame of enthusiasm for the processes of life quenched by soapy water and a drizzly day? It is hard to discover satisfactory answers to why we live without wonder. Daily patterns easily, but not necessarily, fix us into a stereotyped world. We even like to imagine we are not like others who follow an identical pattern. Our little voice within wants to keep some semblance of spiritual vision, so we feel better off than those who wear the same grey clothes as we do.

Neither the human spirit nor any other agency easily shifts us from our fixed ways. An increased restlessness pervading our daily habits generates a struggle to improve our life. Discontent arises at an ignominious way of life. Our daily life is aimless and abstract. We cannot comprehend how our activities, which once seemed innovative, have become meaningless. At this point will-power is still in control, still able to knuckle down and submit obediently to its fate. The inner rebellion can be quelled; conformity and control can still preserve their authority. Yet when we nurture rebellion the opportunity arises to smash unashamedly the mould of mundane values and gain access to greater freedom that cannot be subordinated to social necessities.

When the liberating impulses are granted licence and the rebellion is faithfully nurtured, the potential to move towards a celebratory existence occurs. Realizing the possibility of fresh beginnings we challenge the restrictive myths we hide behind. We confront the oblivion we have put up with, and the spirit triumphs. This spirit and new found passion breaks the shell of dull existence. The heart uplifts into new dimensions with new hopes, but not without pain and risk. We can feel the promise of actualizing potential, but wonder at what cost.

Understanding the source of the potential for change remains something of a mystery. Making the decision to leap into the new vision with the hope of discovery may become simultaneously the joy and torment of existence. However, so doing invites opportunity to experience a limitless perception. This struggle places consciousness in a strange unfamiliar atmosphere. Things are not as fixed as they were. There are new ways to perceive circumstances. The logical, decent and sensible loses the ability to acquiesce to its driven ways.

When we shake off unthinking conformity we are reborn into a greater dimension. We realize the futility of buying into an organized little world. When our heart bursts through these boundaries we touch upon a vision whereby the ordinary falls into place. We experience wonder, touch our deep creative inner resources. However, this does not immediately co-ordinate life into a harmonious and peaceful order. But the dawning of limitless perception honours the human capacity to transcend our limitations, experience a spiritual vibrancy and sense of the Sacred, uninhibited by religious norms. This expands consciousness to such a degree that breaking out of unsatisfactory moulds becomes an expression of human responsibility.

Our daily issues can be viewed with exaltation. These revelations uplift the spirit. We marvel at our ability to view afresh feelings and thoughts from the depths of our being. This now expansive awareness, fascinated by the changes that are taking place, becomes free from death-like existence. We feel receptivity to something other, that before was aloof and thus ignored.

The spiritually vague becomes actual, the spiritually distant becomes intimate. These mystical sensations dance through the inner world into awareness. The ego is dismissed. It bears no significance. We realize we have been carrying around habitual notions of who we think we are. Our roles have defined us and now we have seen through them. Our willingness to actualize our potential, to live in an enlightened way, exults our spirit and pays respect to wisdom.

Our roles and knowledge cannot endure since events supersede them. It requires no obvious conditions for the sudden unearthing of the immensity of the human spirit. It is as if we stumble upon truths about ourselves; about the vast spectrum of life. We realize the Truth of who we think we are is only what we hold onto. Seeing into the Indescribable strips bare our existence. We understand our inability to organize the mind, thoughts and emotions, to generate insights at will. Our receptivity is naturally humble, not born of tackling pride and conceit, nor failure. If we think we are helpless to awaken we subscribe to latent patterns. If we think we can organize our mind to produce insights we are spellbound by mechanistic thought. Any mode of preparation or encouragement seems only to refute spontaneous discovery.

If our efforts to become enlightened are not working, what can we do? Purposeful effort to break out of the conditioned mode—the fire of rebellion against submission—can certainly play a part against a mediocre existence, religious or social. Identification with helplessness works like a guillotine, severing initiative and inquiry into our human condition. The persistence of inner questioning bangs on the door of limitless perceptions.

Time still registers on consciousness with the conventional legitimacy of its comings and goings. Loss of interest in conforming to daily timetables may be upsetting and alarming. We need faith in this silent awareness until the fear of losing touch with the everyday world dispels. Within this unfamiliarity we cut adrift from conventional moorings. We have nowhere to turn, inwardly or outwardly. The familiar that determines who we are and what matters, becomes unfamiliar, even unnecessary. It may be necessary to give up all yearnings to change as our efforts may hinder the flowering of realization. Effort often distracts us from insight. The final recourse is meditative silence where enlightenment can reveal itself. We give ourselves permission to be mindful of That that rests in silence.

Profound meditative silence goes further than telling us something new about ourselves. Such silence confirms a realm without personal considerations. When the mind exhausts its persistent chatter, we fall into silence. Our being empties—revealing a splendour untouched by the passages of time. Raindrops, ideas and fleeting atoms are absorbed into this sacred silence.

This wonderful emptiness is the manna of heaven, the light penetrating through to the ordinary world. It is a mystery that allows revelations to be exposed through its presence. With the fading away of distractions awareness discerns calmness, joy, contentment, single-pointedness and meaningful thought. A spring of happiness radiates through consciousness. The world of things and events recedes slowly without denial or rejection, as this noble silence permeates cellular life. The mind that desires activity diminishes, the urge to make an impact on the world fades into obscurity. Strangely and marvellously, the sense of aliveness within is heightened as awareness surrenders to this silence. Out of this aliveness comes activities expressing a pervasive fullness. The hands in the kitchen sink, the bus queue on the rainy day become revelations from the depths of spiritual realization.

The undirected inner absorption of consciousness gains access to various depths of experience—each noticeably more stabilizing than the previous one. The cells within the body, refine to a degree of subtlety that surpasses physical sensation. This exposes a refined inner vibration, a quiet pulse of life, a faint expansion and contraction taking place. This is formless; the form of the body has faded away into fluctuating atoms, the shape of sights and sound have lost all semblance of thingness and yet the sense of the Here and Now is immensely alive.

In such absorptions this refined awareness senses something awesome, breathtaking in its possibility. It is as though the consecration of absorption blurs together the sweetness of joy and murmurs of fear—revealing a pervasive sense of things. This exposure to the Emptiness of our conventional mind takes our breath away. All that was something is relative after all; conversely what was interpreted as nothing is Profound. The destructuring of the familiar and unfolding of inner absorption exposes a flawless, deathless realm.

Authentic enlightenment influences daily perception and actions. The world of different things is no longer presumed to be ultimately real. The world of things and description belong to relative truth. Enlightenment devastates the structures of conventional life and exorcises the ghosts of time. Our lives become joyful and balanced; active compassion develops spontaneously. We are free and we live that freedom.

CHAPTER TWENTY-FIVE

THE FINAL FREEDOM

Our political leaders can offer us a relative freedom. Those who regard themselves as the guardians of Western democracy tell us we live in the free world. We have the right to vote, to worship, to support and express the ideologies of particular political and religious groups. We also have the freedom to act in ways that suit self-interest, providing it is within the framework of the law. We are indoctrinated into democratic selfishness. These freedoms cherished and upheld from one generation to another stand in stark contrast to people from other regions who are without human rights. So the world is divided into the free world and everywhere else.

Conventional belief in God tacitly supports the political and religious ideologies of the free world. We believe that God is on our side. We believe in the right to protect and defend our democratic institutions with every means at our disposal. We suppress doubts about whether we are free, even at the conventional level. Crime, violence, poverty, corruption, pollution, alcohol, drugs, and unhappiness are common currencies in our society. The authenticity of our values and freedom goes unquestioned. We live in a pathetic fiction of freedom, based on political and financial structures that disregard deeper values and spirituality.

Rhetoric about freedom restricts inquiry into freedom.
The political-religious rhetoric about the "free world" inhibits our interest in a genuine freedom from selfishness, aggression and fear. Our freedom has become restricted to knowing what we want, going after it, and using people and resources to attain it. This behaviour endorses the view that freedom is bound up with

self-interest. Law and order has become a yardstick for what is socially acceptable. One of our primary efforts is getting away with as much as possible this side of the law. In practice, we bend and manipulate the law for personal ends rather than treat it as one of the vehicles of ethical action.

Nobody questions self-interest, denies its expression, or hinders its pursuit. We go after what we want because that is what it means to live in a free society. Yet this aberration of freedom can occur only at the expense of the underclasses and the poor regions of our world. The freedom to accumulate prosperity and prestige succeeds largely at the expense of the "not-free world." We have elevated this fundamental right to exist for personal ends into a metaphysical realm. We think we always know what's best for all of us without considering the interdependent nature of things. We have become a product of our past conditioning and rhetoric; we are agents for global conflicts and destructiveness.

People with a genuine concern for freedom work for social and environmental justice. Acts of reverence for the Earth and its people are often marginalized as the behaviour of militants. Campaigns for justice are permitted providing they do not interfere with the ideology of self-interest and our corrupt democratic institutions. Chained to desire, influential forces for profit dominate society. Money rules supreme in the cult of consumerism. Money is God. The voice of authentic freedom questions the rhetoric. We let go and share rather than pursue and grasp.

Obsession with personal desires restricts freedom.
I am free to do as I please is the cry of the conditioned. Compliance with the values of our self-centred culture means we consume and are consumed by our social environment. External standards and values are useful when they encourage us to consider ourselves in relationship to others. Until all relationships matter equally, we are blind to the impact our desires have upon others and the environment.

We must drop the conventional notion that we live in a free society. Then we may experience the dissatisfaction of our imprisonment to the dominant values of that society. Once we recognize this situation we will decide to do something about it, We look together into ways to explore and express the deep significance of selflessness. We dispense with the creation of heroes and villains as such figures belong to a society living in myths. Such people are a product of society's unresolved inner needs. Our values are concerned with happiness and suffering.

Our blind acceptance of authority restricts our freedom.

Realizing that clinging to religious or political ideology is not the route to freedom, we inquire. Do we want to be free? Who can stop this movement to the final Freedom. In the world of profit and privilege, the dispossessed, animals and nature are relegated to the lower divisions of consideration. They hardly merit a few seconds on prime-time television or in prime-time thoughts. The establishment, including political and religious leaders, functions on rhetoric rather than personal sacrifice, selflessness and sustained contact with people in pain. The privileged spend years in office hardly bothering to visit suburbs of suffering in their own cities. Society has come to consist of the great and the insignificant, the memorable and the irrelevant; most leaders want to be associated with the former and avoid the latter. Compassion has become rhetoric.

We must lose interest in the belief systems that support selfish freedoms and selfish democracy. We regard the political "stars" of this dream world as being rather farcical, sad caricatures of potentially noble people. It is a significant freedom to renounce the awe created around so-called success models and heroes. However, utopia is not around the corner. Projections of power onto authority figures says little about Reality. Investigating these projections helps end the envy and adulation. Once free from the shadow of conventional authority, we can discover how to participate in circumstances with awareness and wisdom.

We restrict our freedom to spiritual forms or the formless.

Our interest then shifts from the material and social worlds to the spiritual. We regard spiritual practices as vehicles in our quest for freedom. It is all too easy for spiritual forms to become an appendix to the main activities of our life. We think saying prayers, meditating a little, attending services and doing good deeds are the essence of the spiritual life. The song of spiritual liberation and awakening requires the spirit to realize and respond to the nature of things.

A story from India points out the relativity of religious practices used to overcome the belief that something is inherently wrong with us. A man convinced himself he had a flea wandering around inside his head. He was serious about this bizarre idea. He could feel the flea crawling around his brain. It was driving him crazy. He called upon a number of wise people who told him: "There is no flea. You are a free human being." He disagreed. They told him that he imagined the presence of the flea. But he could not accept what he heard. One day he came across a homeless soul who wisely said: "Ah yes, you have a flea. What I suggest is that you take this medicine of mindfulness and awareness to watch the path of the flea. Eventually it will come out of your ear." The man with the imaginary flea believed what he heard. The homeless one took a flea from his clothes and secretly held it to the man's ear. "Ah here it is. The flea just crawled down the side of your brain and out of your ear." The man experienced joy and gratitude. "I'm free. I'm free at last."

When our imagination convinces us about something we may need to employ imagination to dissolve the matter. Form and formless spiritual teachings have no special in-built merit to them. Someone engaged in spiritual activity may dissolve the thought of not being free. A new thought "I am free" replaces the old thought. The person then regards the method as the intermediary between the two forms of experience. What is the difference between being tied to the thought "I am free" and tied to the thought "I am not free?" What insight will liberate us from clinging to either side of this duality?

We restrict freedom through our views.
We perceive the world and the meaning of life in countless ways. To be stuck with the view that life is suffering is the philosophy of despair. It can also lead to hoping for a blissful state, a heavenly kingdom or an unchanging Self. Self wants Nirvana, or God, so that this painful world will go away or become "lila", a spiritual play. Or we claim life is a wonderful creation but then we are haunted with fear of personal extinction.

Are we willing to dump these packaged views? Are we interested in freedom from the countless views about existence, the nature of self and the world? We are arrogant when we champion our beliefs. We can ask ourselves why we stubbornly shine our spiritual light in front of others, and discover that what we get from our self satisfied spirituality is power. Spiritual experiences and their resultant ideologies exert power over others. But if we become infatuated with this power, our cognitions only lead to the fixation of viewpoints and reinforcement of duality.

Methods, techniques and forms have no inherent value nor does absence of them. We impose value on form or the formless or both. We often take up the formless approach when we convince ourselves of the limitation of spiritual practices. We proclaim a formless spirituality through rejection of form. Or we proclaim form through the rejection of a formless spirituality. Conclusions about form or the formless are wrapped up in thoughts. Infinite Freedom is a total waking-up to the nature of things, not a confinement to form or the formless.

Freedom knows no measurement.

In noble silence, when our brain is still, we experience a realm that liberates the interdependent connection with all things. Our saving grace is liberation from infatuation with any cognitions of mind. Awareness possesses no inherent essence but is connected to experiences, ideas and things. Conventional truths consist of a variety of agreements and disagreements locked into each other. Digging a position, is exhausting. Spiritual utopias in this world or any other belong to religious fantasy life.

The passion to uphold personal, social and religious myths has gone. We realize we are not left with something or nothing but with this utterly relevant Emptiness that leaves us wordless. People may tell us we are thoughtful, or are dedicated to deep values. But these descriptions have no meaning, for the Truth of things cannot be confined to definitions of meaning. Freedom offers joy and expansive wonder as we realize an immeasurable enlightenment.

The love of Freedom includes questioning freedoms we believe we already have.

The love of Freedom includes the ability to give up both what is unsatisfactory and satisfactory.

The love of Freedom includes the renunciation of clinging to spiritual standpoints.

The love of Freedom includes wisdom in the face of appearances, duality and struggle.

The love of Freedom sees the emptiness of power and self proclama-

tion.
The love of Freedom celebrates the realization that this world is not as it appears to be and that it is not otherwise.
The love of Freedom responds to voices of dissatisfaction.
The triumph of Freedom is that it is indestructible.
Free, Free, Free at last.

CHAPTER TWENTY-SIX

THIS ECSTACY OF NO INHERITANCE

Wisdom is not prepared to submit. Relentless social messages distract sincere spiritual exploration. We realize that the mind-and-body does not belong to us or to anyone else but is a form of life. We have rejected current models of success, secular or religious. They bear no relationship to the way we feel about things. We have understood that liberation and our natural reverence for life means everything to us, with implications for the rest of existence. This daily participation is the expression of something unspeakable that fills our awareness.

Ultimate Truth soaks perceptions and what we perceive. To marginalize spirituality is profane. We refuse to treat it as an appendix to the mainstream of our daily life. A few intimate friends also appreciate this timeless liberation or the opportunity for its realization. Other friends concentrate their attention on the everyday stuff of conventional matters, while some keep a safe distance from digging into the soul of things, except perhaps when faced with some temporary crisis.

We can share our spiritual sensitivities and insights with those unfamiliar with such experiences. It is not that we purposefully cultivate, or want to claim a spiritual identity, but we know we taste something Inexpressible. We have no doubts about that. Our experiences confirm that we cannot return to the old socially conditioned patterns. We had never been wholeheartedly in favour of them, and now we have awakened to something of a different dimension. We have also felt a quality of undeniable happiness that has swept away a lifetime of concern with personal choices and needs. What we feel and what we know fuse.

We have examined the religion of our birth with an open

mind. Our motives were to see what was common between this spiritual awakening and our former religion. Understanding that prejudgments hindered genuine interest, we enter spiritual inquiry with a quality of innocence. We have not wished to discredit, but we have often kept hitting the same barrier—that religion is inseparable from adherence to a founder, text or tradition. Yet we must acknowledge that there are people of orthodox religious beliefs who show immeasurable love and compassion. Warmed by their faith, we continue to be respectful to their expression of a religious faith. But we have restrained from total participation in its ways.

Various edicts of religion seem to have become over time etched in stone. Making contact with liberated voices within a religion requires determination. These outspoken ones, who wish to breathe a new lease of life into a faith dying on its feet, are increasing. But they know that making changes through a more relevant message does not lie at the core of spirituality. Preoccupation with preservation of the old tradition or modernizing it, fails to penetrate to the depth of spiritual awakening. At times, we sense formal religion offers its members Band-Aids when the faithful need oxygen.

We have felt commensurate with many religious values, but we care not an iota for dogmatism. Our statements of disbelief are often unacceptable to the legions of religious devotees, but we cannot compromise our spiritual experiences. Heart-transforming revelations have no conceptual source leaving nothing to fashion a religious position upon.

Our religious experience becomes a statement of disbelief:

I do not believe there is any reality which created it and loves it.

I do not believe in prayer to an ultimate being.

I do not believe that there is a book that has any unique spiritual significance.

I do not believe that it matters how the world began or how it will end.

I do not believe there is any transcendent or human force that will determine the future of the world.

I do not believe any individual claimants to Truth or enlightenment warrant worship or devotion.

I do not believe that I should persuade myself to adopt others' beliefs because of what they tell me.

I do not believe that I have to rely upon myself or another.
I do not have to make this statement into a set of beliefs.

With a firm stroke of the pen, we can declare our authentic will and testament. It is our magnum opus, not the voice of defiance in rage against others, but a contemporary testimony of witness, an experience and Truth, via negation of belief. We can experience more than relief in this statement of honesty. We can taste a spiritual liberation. The first and last priority, the heart of the spiritual life, are our insights into the experience of the Profound. Separation from the Profound condemns us to a profane existence. This statement of disbelief does not threaten daily happiness nor isolate us from the world around. The converse is true. Disregard for beliefs and dogmatic views exposes a certitude that was previously obscure.

Proclamations of beliefs of the conditioned self form a religion. Though a religion may point towards divine experiences and away from the crass consumer culture, it is not enough. The authentic religious message is like a boat. What is important is to experience the destination, not to spend life at sea. A boundless joy, an undiluted wonder pervade the deep recesses of existence when a human being is not bound to conditioning. To cross the sea to the far shore is the heart of the matter, not the condition of the ship.

A faultless realization does not declare fixed beliefs, nor propound any position. To proselytize a position of non-position would be ludicrous. That would sabotage the statement of disbelief. Anything we identify with might sound like the early stages of a religious doctrine or a poorly defined theology that a religious scholar could rip apart. To pay full respect to Ultimate Truth requires cessation of religion and all names and forms. Truth does not require missionaries. The wise speak that which is true *and* useful. By adopting this pragmatic standpoint we trust people to sense in some mysterious way that the expression of a realized life is different and has something meaningful to communicate.

Initially, our silence seems to protect ultimate discovery but the notion of protection of Ultimate Truth is absurd. Absorption into the mystery of things through a palpable silence breaks the spell of a defined consciousness. Our religion is awareness. What matters is full realization, not the voyage. Realization embraces the world of Here and Now, this and that, the near and far shore. Experiences, reflections, readings and spiritual journeys become revelations of this timeless abiding. The wise, mystics, and poets have made observations that speak directly of an enlightened life. There is no certitude that those who wrote such gems deeply comprehend their own words, but it does not matter. Gems come out of the blue. There is no need to construct models of spirituality; that would be a desecration of spontaneous insights.

Any attempt to organize the Truth defies the Truth. Any claims that Truth constructs or deconstructs, is ancient or post-modern, are born from those who use their brains to analyse. They have adopted a conceived world, and have gained their reputation as conceivers. Subjective and objective perceptions make up a conceived existence and a constructed world. Truth cannot be caged in language games. Liberating insights humble life rendering the brain cells silent.

Exposure to the nature of things reveals more than what is obvious. The world is like a magical garden, full of inexhaustible secrets. Paradoxically, we know that we do not know and we do not know what we know. In an extraordinary manner, happiness soaks perceptions whenever we attempt to make sense of ultimacy. In the midst of contact with the nature of things, there is not only peace but the manifestation of a wry humour. The inability to explain, to fathom the unfathomable, leaves heartfelt amusement at the unhinged Truth.

Realization of Ultimate Truth dissolves the appetite for the conceiver and the conceived. It is the conceived truth that triggers the outpourings of faith and doubt and the potential for inflamed beliefs. There is no location for the "I" in Ultimate Truth nor even in conceived views; thus no place is left for conceit. We become aware of how easy it is to dismiss others who champion their conceptions of Truth in the arena of public debate. The Ultimate and Inconceivable Truth blows away the cobwebs of ego.

Since we cannot assume to possess Truth, we express an unassuming nature. Personality and activities express realizations. There is a certain enigma about the enlightened beings that often leave others with a sense of curiosity, if not wonder. All people and things are inseparably intimate with the symphony of Truth. Those who conceive that enlightened ones possess the Ultimate Truth and others do not speak from the standpoint of the conventional mind. We can smile when we hear such convictions of the everyday mind.

Ultimate Truth has not been set up for dealing with the conventional truths or for the protection of anybody. It was not established for the benefit of a knower, to form a position, nor to create spiritual teachings. Ultimate Truth is not an object that can be pursued nor defined. It possesses no mark, no signs, no characteristics and abides unobstructed. Suffering has no foothold in Ultimate Truth. These realizations influence morality, meditation and wisdom. The Ultimate is like a banana tree that has no centre yet it reveals leaves.

Enlightenment is incomprehensible.

Enlightenment reveals lack of self existence and egotism.

Enlightenment ends belief in separation and oneness.

Enlightenment cannot be found outside of any relationship.

Enlightenment cannot be found through another person or self.

Enlightened person or self is a concept in enlightenment.

Enlightenment is not what it appears to be and not otherwise.

Enlightenment does not possess inherent existence.

Conceptions of existence do not possess enlightenment.

There is no enlightenment in enlightenment.

There is no centre, no reference point. In the old days before spiritual enlightenment, the seeker imagined that he or she would have to work hard to end the unsatisfactory patterns that affected the quality of his or her life. In full spiritual realization no production or continuity takes place. What has not started does not have to be stopped. Patterns have no inherent existence to them so there is nothing there of substance to let go of, negate or surrender. The Profound and the profane are inseparable. Incompletion and completion, development and perfection, surrender and grace, have no inherent relevance. Ultimately, to apprehend anyone as superior or inferior, courageous or fearful is a cocktail of conceited views. It is a made-up world.

Enlightenment reveals that there is no position to stand on, not inside Truth, nor outside it, nor in between. Ultimately neither questions nor answers have more significance. Profound questions about life may generate insights, or render silence, or the question is the answer.

What is this rejoicing with nothing
To rejoice over,
This ecstasy of no inheritance,
This enchantment that cannot explain itself?
What is this in which neither coming from,
Nor going to nor standing still
Has any relevance?
Let us not forget THAT which is unspeakable.